PUSH
HIP HOP HISTORY
THE
BROOKLYN SCENE
BY Mabusha Cooper

Educated Voices of Hip Hop

THE AUTHOR AND EDITORS
THANK THE FOLLOWING PEOPLE
FOR THEIR HELP IN THE CREATION OF THIS BOOK.

The Standard Family
Rosalyn Gilmore
Pleshette Moore
The Cooper Family
Strafe
7 DS
Skeeter
Lumumba Carson
David Black
Dave Parrish Steez of Culture
Fab 5 Freddy
Criss Cross and BSD
Leo Cato
Kevin W. Porter
Ralph Cassanova
Phase 2
James
Tuesday Thomas
Fritz Jean
Jimmy Spicer
Wayne Winston

Dahza
Dawoud Bey
Troy McCune
Stan 153
P. Ryan
H.O.P.
Chain 3
Boodah Bros
D Mecca
T.F.G.
The Flower Family
The Plummer Family
Shola Akintlayo
Nucleus (Newcleus)
Icast
88 Hip Hop
Renegade
Adele Premice
Bete
Iron Mike Tyson
Brenda Connor-Bey

Special Thanks to Our Editor Heather Stiell.
Special Thanks to our designers:
Camille, Tulio, Gilbert and Wesley of S&S Graphics

EXCERPTS FROM
AN INTRODUCTION TO THE BLACK CONTRIBUTION
TO THE DEVELOPMENT OF BROOKLYN

INTRODUCTION

Brooklyn's history is comparable to a rich multi-colored fabric that represents her folklore, historic events, outstanding personalities, and progressive movements.

EARLY BROOKLYN

In 1645 Breuckelen Villiage was founded by the Dutch. By 1660 all of the six original towns that formed what is now known as Kings County had received their patents. Although many of the Blacks brought to New Netherland were slaves, some were free citizens as early as 1633. The free Blacks were landowners and prosperous members of the community. Due to a shortage of Black women, some Black male settlers married rich Dutch women. These Blacks were accorded full rights and privileges as citizens under the Dutch and for at least fifty years after the English conquered New Netherland.

Successful BUSINESS MEN, Brooklyn, N.Y.

SLAVERY

1619 marked the introduction of slavery to the New World. Prior to 1645 slavery was unknown to Blacks who resided in Breuckelen and other towns known as Kings County. After 1665 when the English conquered New Netherland, slaves were reduced to chattels by the English in 1702 under the "Black Codes". By 1790 Kings County was the largest slave-holding county in New York State.

COMMUNITIES

Within the civil divisions called the Ninth Ward were small concentrations of Blacks in settlements that emerged in the 1830's and disappeared around 1880. The remaining Blacks formed the nucleus of Black Bedford-Stuyvesant. After the Black migrations from the South during the twentieth century, Brooklyn became the largest Black community in America.

Published by
<u>New Muse Community Museum of Brooklyn- 1977</u>

THE BROOKLYN SCENE

It is somewhat difficult to introduce the underground Brooklyn Hip Hop movement to you, the reader, since Brooklyn's contributions to the development of this unique culture are rarely heard of. When we hear of "Hip Hop pioneers," we immediately think of greats like Kool Here, Afrika Bambaataa and CrazyLegs (all from the Bronx); we never associate pioneers with Brooklyn. One may not readily attribute the "electric boogie" or "pop locking" of today to dance styles that emerged on the West coast (with Don Cambell's Lockers) in the 1970's. Neither does one easily recognize the tenacity of Sha-rock (Bronx), the first female MC, as the rungs of the ladder upon which future generations of female hip hop artists (MC Lyte, Queen Latifah, Lil's Kim) climbed to success. This text's purpose is in no way to cause any division in the culture of Hip Hop; however, the intention is to document key periods in the evolutionary process of the sound system with a centralized focus on Brooklyn, while pinpointing the various style elements of this cultural development in the boroughs of New York. My main objective is to place the pieces of this elaborate puzzle together, by entering the minds of illustrious personalities to learn their love of Brooklyn and of the Hip Hop art form.

I had the extraordinary experience in the 1970's to be exposed to and become a part of this culture in it purest form-raw, without the synthetic commercialization that tends to dilute all forms of art. Before Rap was recorded on records and Breakin' went to the big screen. Hip Hop contains a number of elements that contribute to its vibrant being, such as DJing, Masters of Ceremonies (MCing), graffiti, idiom, fashion and many more. The culture itself has no boundaries. In Hip Hop there is no absolute, only an incipient, never ending cycle mediated by socioeconomic state, political consciousness or deviancy.

Brooklyn (Kings County), the borough of churches, was the birthplace of the monster sound system and home of the famous Caribbean Day parade. In the 1960's, through ghetto code, an alternative style of communication, Brooklyn natives began referring to the borough as "the hood" (short for neighborhood), a term that would be adopted a decade later in inner cities across America. When the Civil Rights movement came to a close, unemployment in Black and Latino communities throughout the inner city was at an all-time high. There was a concurrent rise in gang activity. Gangs residing in New York -- such as the Nomads, Jollystompers, Hellcats and Black Spades -- emerged as coping structures, havens for youth otherwise disempowered by a stifling political and economic atmosphere. The movement to the streets was a reclamation of space outside of social confines, and each gang marked its turf with colorful emblems that were signifiers of its unique presence, slowly giving birth to a new cultural movement, an incredible art form which was the manifestation of resistance among oppressed inner city youth.

Decorative gang jackets and other unique paraphernalia of that era would gradually materialize into breakdance crew colors. Horrific gang fights would be replaced by creative, energetic dance bouts, arbitrated by a DJ armed with an arsenal of records.

At this juncture, the early 1970's, artists such as the late Grandmaster Flowers, Pete DJ Jones, DJ Maboya, the late DJ Ron Plummer, MC KC The Prince of Soul, Smith Brothers, Action Jackson and so many more unsung heroes were laying the foundation for the surging Hip Hop scene. However, DJ Slash (aka Mahoney) of Brooklyn vividly recalled that music bands were the first source of entertainment at block parties and the DJs would come later. Disco B, an original DJ from Brooklyn, strongly believes that Flowers from Brooklyn and Pete DJ Jones, of the Bronx, were founding fathers of the "mix". Unfortunately, some Hip Hop pioneers criticize this theory, classifying the two as prominent DJs of the mainstream disco era. Still, other DJs from the early 1970's maintain that Pete and Flowers played all types of music, not just disco. Thus, heated debates exist in the Hip Hop community as to the validity of various accounts of Hip Hop culture's historical development.

During the same period, the media discovered the Harlem and Bronx crews which featured artists such as Eddie Chiba, Phase 2, Luv Bug Starski, Kurtis Blow, Hollywood, Grandmaster Flash and Busy Bee. Although isolated from the media hype, Brooklyn's underground movement grew quietly and swiftly. Graffiti writers like Ex-Vandals, The God Squad, Vanguards, Flint, Jamestop, X men, Dondi, Dust, Burn and 7 Deadly Sins hit the train yards and walls, while Smiz 1 and the Gnome Kraftwork beautified the handball courts. Breakdance groups like Rock with Style, Another Bad Creation (A.B.C.), Majestic Rockers, Fresh Kids and the Furious Rockers would develop impeccable reputations as dancers. At the amazing park jams or center jams, one could witness a favorite DJ "cut up" records without headphones. After the introduction to headphones, many DJs who could not afford headphones used telephone receivers to cue records. A new, ingenious and adaptive cultural phenomena, Hip Hop was transcendent all over New York.

In comparison to the Bronx back then, we can not neglect that Brooklyn artists lacked a cohesiveness with each other. Kool Here and Afrika Bambaataa, two dynamic DJs, had been able to organize much of the Bronx Hip Hop community into one group. Master Jay & Michael Dee's 1980 recording of The Sounds of Brooklyn, "T.S.O.B.," closely resembled an organizational rallying cry for Brooklyn, though Brooklyn youth would later organize under a different banner. As this street culture began to mature, terminology and style evolved differently from county to county. For example, within the breakdancing element, many dancers in-

BKLYN

Brooklyn referred to breakin' as free styling or rockin'. In the Bronx, the term "B-boying" was synonymous with breakin' (dancing) or representing oneself as a breaker, whereas to Brooklyn residents it embodied attitude and a style of dress. Still, certain parts of New York had various definitions of B-boys. In some neighborhoods, the term was a short translation for "Banji Boys," who were known to disrupt parties.

Around this time, the late 1970's and early 1980's, many low income juvenile delinquent males, disconnected from schools and families, embraced a deviant lifestyle opposing mainstream society as "the haves" and themselves as the "have nots". In the community, these youth offenders were known as hard rocks because of their dress and their lack of respect for authority. They wouldn't wear belts with their pants, so their pants would sag, and their sneakers stayed untied--both of which symbolized the plight of incarceration. Eventually, these were incorporated into a B-boy look, whose signature would remain as the foundation and epitome of hard-core hip hop fashion. The B-boy female counterpart, fashion conscious teenage girls, were known as B-girls or "Boosters," an elitist breed of shoplifters. A small number of delinquents from various neighborhoods in the county, like Bed Stuy, Fort Greene, Brownsville, Bushwick and East New York, were in the process of organizing and creating the infamous "bum rush", a distinctive method of assault and robbery committed by a group of destructive youth. Tabloid newspapers would receive their first taste of the dreadful act in the early 1980's, at Diana Ross' free concert in Central Park, where the mobs went on a chain- and purse-snatching spree. The news media called the mobs "wolf packs" and would later rename the criminal offense "wilding", fostering a criminal representation of the borough, and painting a permanent picture particularly within Hip Hop. New York City youth would select character names that would serve as identifiers of their respective boroughs. Brooklyn was known as "Crooklyn", Manhattan as "Money Makin", Bronx as "The Boogie Down", Queens as "the Bridge" (short for Queens Bridge) and Staten Island, "the Island".

NYC

In 1986, recording artist KRS One/Boogie Down recorded " The Bridge Is Over" his controversial rebuttal to MC Shan's The Bridge". KRS lyrical assault , " Manhattan keeps on making it, Brooklyn keeps on taking' it, the Bronx Keeps on creating it, and Queens keeps on faking it, " would ignite a series of borough rivalries through Rap songs. These conflicts remained on vinyl, which, for that time period, demonstrated extremely good sportsmanship and the importance of establishing one's dominance in the emergent and yet uncharted Hip Hop scene. Nearly ten years later, the late Notorious B.I.G. would bring the spotlight back to Kings County and refurbish the spirits of our pioneers from all five boroughs, whom Hip Hop historians had abandoned.

I thought my story might lack richness and objectivity if I told it alone, so I interviewed a few artists who narrated their own experience. Brace yourself as we engage in a mental escapade within in the world of the Brooklyn Hip Hop Movement.

L.STANDARD

PUSH (Mabusha Cooper) - 1972

"The promoters could pay less for a DJ than they paid for the bands, so that's why the DJ's became popular"- Strafe

Matthew of the Elusions playing in 1975.

Hip Hop History
The Brooklyn Scene

(Their Own Words)

INTERVIEWS WITH:

JEFF LOVE

DUST

SUPREME

INFINITY

PROFESSOR X (R.I.P.)

KING UPROCK

KWIK STEP

TRON

PETE DJ JONES

TONY PATRICK

JAMESTOP

COSMO

BETE

SCOTCH 79

EX-VANDALS

SHOCK A LOCK

FLINT 707

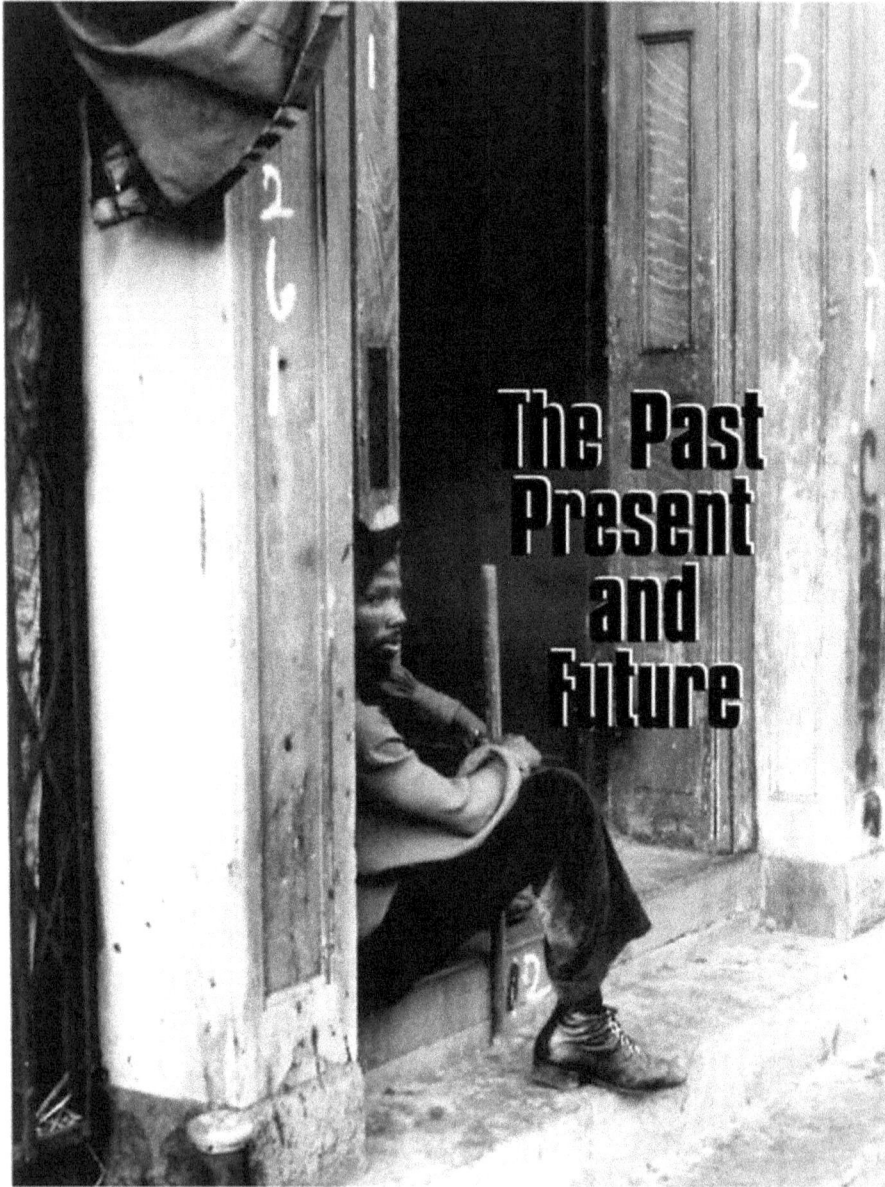

The Past
Present
and
Future

THE SUMMER OF RAP 1968

" We have to consider ourselves the authors of a new justice."

- H. Rap Brown

Photo: Lolita Standard

"Theres A Riot Goin On"
-Sly & The Family Stone

1960's
Brooklyn, NYC

It is a startling fact of the times
we live in that some of the most brilliant, gifted and promising
Black young people in the nation have been driven into
an angry alienation, both repeated and
painful frustrations and disillusinment.

Notes

Hodges,E.W.Norman, Black History, Simion & Schuster,1974
The Family Stone &Sly. "There's A Riot goin on", Epic records, 1971

MICHAEL STEWART
1958-1983

CLINTON HILL

BROOKLYN

THE
spirit
OF
HIP HOP

...JEFF LOVE

THE SPIRIT OF
HIP HOP

Jeff Love aka Meeko Isreal: DJ/poet and former member of W.B.M.J. (Worlds Best Mobile Jockeys)

Push: Can you name some of the members that were in your crew?

Jeff: The founding member was myself, Freddy D who also used to play with Grandmaster Flowers, Franky D from Lafayette Gardens and Matt D, who was the youngest member, he was more technical. We all are from Brooklyn. Also there was a brother called Sugar Bear. In other circles he was known as Gold D.

Push: (laughing) I remember Sugar Bear. I used to get on his nerves

Jeff: Yeah! He was once part of the first record pool, Disco record pool. The leader of that pool was Bert Lumpkin. She was a female DJ.

Push: A female DJ in Brooklyn?

Jeff: No doubt, she was one of the best. She was the first one to get us free records, actually she goes back to the 1960's. When I was born, she was around the Brooklyn bands such as Crown Heights Affair, B.T. Express, and, I think, Brass Construction-- she was doing sound with them. Shortly after, the DJing started coming about.

Push: Wow, that's some history. Now, I want to talk more about the park jams. Your group was notorious for the park jams.

Jeff: Yeah, the park jams get me stopped on the trains, I'm talking about now-- this present day.

Push: Name some of the parks.

Jeff: Fort Greene park, Triangle Park, which is on Eastern Parkway and Washington Ave.-- a lot of DJ's used to play there: Grand Master Flowers, Franky D, even Pete DJ Jones, because a lot of his crew was from Brooklyn. New Park- we used to call New Park Grand Avenue and Gates.

Push: Where they built the condos!

Jeff: Yeah. P.S. 56, P.S. 11-- all these parks were

"We lost the spiritual value of Hip Hop and we're in danger of losing the soul of Hip Hop"

around the same neighborhood. Biggie Smalls, and Dana Dane. All these cats were listening to me spin-- I guess seventeen years ago. We also jammed in Brownsville, Van Dyke Projects.

Push: What was going on in the different boroughs in the 1970's?

Jeff: I think a lot needs to be said about what was going on in the boroughs of the Bronx and Brooklyn in the 1970's. At that time, we [the two boroughs] were both DJing in the park with makeshift speakers, we were both drawing large crowds, we were both learning how to scratch and rap at the same time. It's just weird how they tried to separate the boroughs. It goes back to what the man tries to do all the time, separate, conquer and divide. I think we should recognize that, definitely. When you think about the talent of Pete DJ Jones and Grand Master Flowers, I mean they set the stage for the Disco design for the very spot we're sitting in right now. They paved the way so...we need to spread the props around. That builds unity. It may seem like a small thing, who started it [Hip Hop] and when did it start. It's the unity that matters that's where I'm coming from. Hip Hop was built on mathematics. You can say God, you can say Jesus, you can say Islam -- it was built on strong stuff. Which can go back to our African values. Now that was wiped away by separation like the way they divided Hip Hop by the boroughs. We lost the spiritual value of Hip Hop and we're in danger of losing the soul of Hip Hop.

Push: True... Now let's talk turntables. What type of turntables did you use when you first began DJing?

Jeff: Gerrard's BSR's. Let me break this down, how scratching came about. BSR's were belt drive turntables. It [the turntable] has a rubber band that holds the wheel of steel, so the more you cue, the more the wheel pulls back. When I was down in 1972...

Push: In 1972?

Jeff: 1972! No doubt that's when mobile disco came about. We had no headphone facility: we had one turntable hooked to an amp and the other turntable hooked up to another amp. What we had to do is cue the record, so you had to put your ear down to the turntable and pull back and forward, and back and forward. All the people out there must research, and be able to talk about Hip Hop the way I'm talking now.

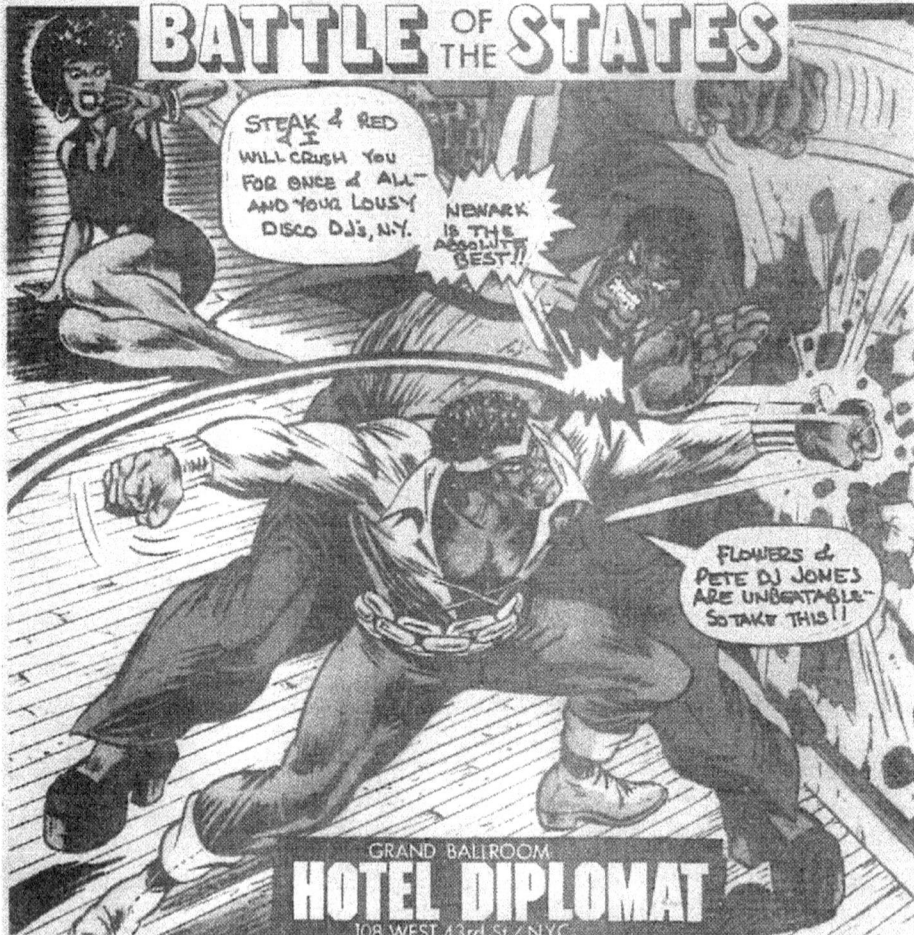

PETE DJ JONES AND GRANDMASTER FLOWERS FLYER

"BROOKLYN REPRESENT Y'ALL"
JAY Z & NOTORIOUS B.I.G
BROOKLYN FINEST

TROUBLE-FREE **BSR** RECORD CHANGER

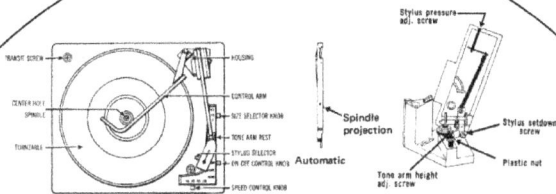

Stylus pressure adj. screw

TRANSIT SCREW
HOUSING
CENTER HOLE
SPINDLE
CONTROL ARM
SIZE SELECTOR KNOB
TONE ARM REST
STYLUS SELECTOR
TURNTABLE
ON-OFF CONTROL KNOB
SPEED CONTROL KNOB

Spindle projection

Automatic

Stylus setdown screw
Plastic nut
Tone arm height adj. screw

OPERATING INSTRUCTIONS

IMPORTANT: Remove all packing material.

A. Float changer by turning transit screws clockwise until fully down against mainplate.

B. Unlock control arm by pressing down at the top rear near the housing and rotate the front free end towards the center of the turntable.

AUTOMATIC PLAY:

1. Insert automatic spindle fully into the center hole by rotating the spindle until side projection is engaged in locking slot.

2. Lift control arm and swing to the right.

3. Stack up to 6 records on center spindle holding the stack with the left hand and position control arm over the records.

4. Select correct stylus.

5. Set selector knobs to correct size and speed.

6. Start unit by sliding control knob from "stop" to "auto" position; hold momentarily until turntable starts to revolve and release gently.

7. To reject records, repeat step "6."

8. After last record, tone arm will return to its rest and unit will shut off automatically.

SEMI-AUTOMATIC PLAY:

1. Lift control arm and swing to right, leave in that position.

2. Place record on turntable.

3. Slide control knob from "stop" to "auto" position, and let it gently return to "start."

4. Stylus will set down on record and will repeat play automatically when record ends.

5. For automatic shut-off, after stylus sets down, gently return control arm to center and lower. Tone arm will return to rest at end of record and unit will shut-off.

ADJUSTMENTS: This changer has been accurately preadjusted to correct stylus set down, stylus pressure and tone arm height. If new adjustments should ever be necessary, make them as follows:

Use flat BSR-PSB99 adaptor spindle to play 45 rpm records.

KEEP THIS INSTRUCTION DISC FOR REFERENCE

TDC-129   Printed in U.S.A.
                          500M-172

STYLUS PRESSURE: This adjustment should only be made with a suitable stylus pressure gauge. Turn stylus pressure adjusting screw clockwise to reduce stylus pressure; counterclockwise to increase pressure.

STYLUS SET-DOWN: Adjust with set-down screw to position stylus 1/8" from record edge at start. Turn screw clockwise to move stylus towards record edge. Counterclockwise to move stylus towards record center.

TONE ARM HEIGHT: To raise, hold plastic nut firmly and turn tone arm height adjustment screw, by hand, counter-clockwise. To lower, turn screw head clockwise. Correct setting is when tone arm clears top of arm rest by 1/8"

TRANSIT INSTRUCTIONS:

1. Lock tone arm in support rest and tie with string.

2. Turn transit screws counterclockwise until changer mainplate is firmly down against motor board.

3. Lock control arm by depressing the top rear near the housing and rotate the free end to the right until it locks.

HIP HOP INFLUENCES

On The Subway

the last poets

JAMES BROWN
THE LAST POETS
GIL SCOTT HERON
JOCKO
AND MANY MORE..........

MC KC Prince Of Soul with Pete DJ Jones

Brooklyn Bronx all city DJ team.

DJ Mocha
Sunflower on the mix 1999

Catchin'

...Dust

Catchin' Wreck

Dust: Artist, B-boy, one of the founders of 7D.S. (7 Deadly Sins) Graffiti crew. "We were basically IND wreckers"

Push: **Let's get your history down first. When did you start writing?**

Dust: I started writing in 1972, then I started bombing-- actually hitting the trains-- from 1976 to 1981. That's when we started wrecking it, me and my crew, my man Kilo, Lil' Star, BM3, Biz Bid, Ac. Oh, it was a bunch of us [graffiti writers], my man Dion5, and then we hooked up with Tor, T.D.4., Un, Shick, NA Rock, T.D.C., T.N.S. It was whole bunch of us bombing.

Push: **What was the name of your particular crew?**

Dust: Definitely 7D.S.

Push: **How did you get that name and why?**

Dust: One day we all were hanging out and we needed a crew; and so my man Tor thought of Seven Deadly Sins, because it was a Rock record and I think the name of the group was Lust. So we **all** said to Tor, "yo, that's a good name," because I was a DJ back then. I was known as Dynasty back then, and boom- that's how everything went down. The name was S.D.S. and Tor said make it 7D.S. and that's how it went down.

Push: **What time era are we talking about?**

Dust: Right there we're talking 1976.

Push: **What train lines were you guys hitting?**

Dust: We were rocking the "ding dongs," any train that went *(ding dong)*.

Push: **[Pausing to laugh] So you were "all city" writers?**

Dust: All city means you're hitting every line from IRT, BMT, to IND lines. We were basically IND
wreckers, you know what I'm saying? We would wreck the IND because that was our home
line, so that was the [train] line we took charge of and we wrecked them from 1976 to 1981,
non-stop. Anyone who came on that line had to get off! That's how it when down.
Only a couple of people [graffiti writers] had hanging out cars like T.N.S., T.D.4.

Push: What about the female graffiti writers?

Dust: Oh man, we had a lot of female writers. We had Lady Shock, Shos, SS Chick, Loving, Loving 2 and Heart. There are other females a lot of people don't want to give no love to: Female Heart, Web, Dimples, Tracey would hit with Demo from Queens (NY). We had females down with us especially SS, Chick and Shota from C.I.A.

Push: Why didn't Brooklyn crews receive the same type of recognition as crews from other boroughs in New York City?

Dust: Brooklyn always takes charge! I think this was a way for the Bronx and Manhattan crews to try to say they put graffiti on the map and we all know it started (in Brooklyn) at the same time. It was all part of the culture, all part of what we call Hip Hop culture.

Push: No doubt.

Dust: If you're an artist, I don't see how can you originate something. What an artist does is reflect what's around him, so I don't know how you can say you originate something. Do you know what I'm saying?

Push: True

Dust: An artist reflects what he sees...you know, I get a little upset when Bronx and Manhattan crews disrespect people from Brooklyn and give us no love. They know about Brooklyn graffiti crews like C.I.A., 7D.S., T.D.4, S.C.B., ROK, SNAK, TROY. They don't give these brothers no love and they were the ones wrecking- Duro and Dondi. Basically, they gave Dondi more love than any of the graffiti writers from this side of town. I never understood why, since we were all down with each other and we were all down with the culture.

Push: What was that whole scene like, bombing on the trains in the train yards?

Dust: Pure adrenaline! It was crazy! That's what a lot of people don't understand, like some writers of today. They say that they're graffiti writers, but they never understood what it was like to stay in a subway tunnel and almost get hit by an express train. Pure adrenaline. You had to look out for other graff crews you had beef with, keep a look out for the Graffiti Task Force and John the Cop. Yo, it was real hectic in the train lay up and if you did have beef with another crew you always had to be on point, you know what I'm saying?

When we had a train lay up we ran, it was Fort Hamilton. We ran that tunnel--nobody was going in there, only through us. If you went in our lay up you had to sneak in there between 1976 to 1981. All the graffiti writers in New York knew that. At one time, the lay up was so underground, people were wondering where and how we were hitting those trains. Another thing too, is back then when we were inside bombers [writers] we used to wreck the inside of the train, totally take charge of the inside of the train. We were about bombing. You had these other writers that would do top to bottoms and their burners. Sometimes they would spend two to three days on the same car doing their work..

Push: **What about school?**

Dust: School? In school they didn't provide us with any programs! So we had to get our groove on. Man, when those graffiti writers got into those galleries they opened a can of worms, they let the New York City Transit Authority know how it was going down. I myself was asked plenty of times to do some shows in the gallery. Like I told you before, we (7D.S.) were a crew that wanted to bomb. It wasn't about getting and being commercial!

Push: **So do you think graffiti has been exploited by mainstream society?**

Dust: Sure!

Push: **Where is graffiti now?**

Dust: Well now that graffiti is worldwide, it has evolved considerably. You now have brothers doing miraculous stuff with spray cans, cnvas, on walls, and I give them the props. The difference between now and then is that then, you couldn't do that on a train, you always had to catch your back. That's what was really about. You had to defeat the time element around you like the police, your enemies...this would really define a true graffiti artist. Now graffiti is everywhere, but even back then we had all types of nationalities. Me personally, I even knew an Indian writer. You had Puerto Ricans, Blacks-everybody was catching wreck on the trains. Brothers were getting down for their crown, but we all know it started in New York-graffiti is part of the Hip Hop movement. We showed society that we are articulate and wise, we showed the world (that] in poverty you do have creativity!

DUST 7DS
BK ORIGINAL

"It's the unity that matters that's where I'm coming from"- Jeff Love

Burns & Dust 7DS Graff Kings of the Ding Dong trains.

"No one DJ can take claim for starting Hip Hop."
- Pete DJ Jones

A Cool Cat, Shandu and Divine on St. Johns Place, Brooklyn, New York.

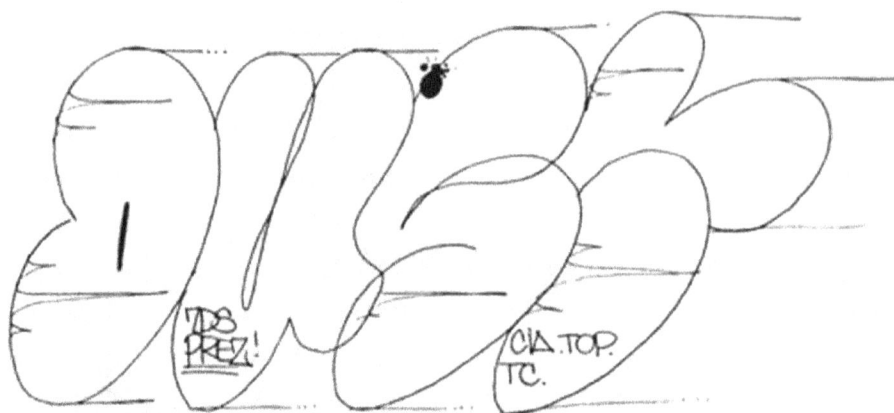

On The 1's and 2's

Suprep

"We used to put sewing needles in the BSR's"

Supreme:
(Shack Crew, House of Power)
Pop Locker Dancer, Host and DJ.

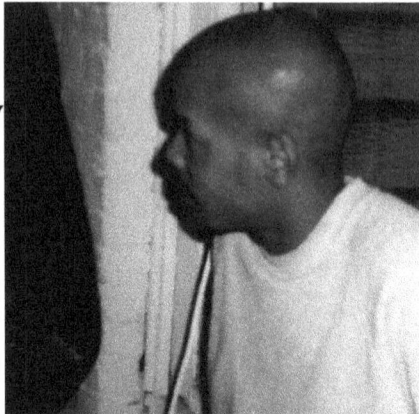

Push: **What area of Brooklyn are you From?**

Supreme: Bed Stuy! You might as well say born and raised. I've been living here for 25 years and now I'm thirty. Brooklyn bred, Bed Stuy is my home.

Push: **When did you start dancing?**

Supreme: Well I really started DJing first, in the mid 1970's, but I went to dancing because I was better at dancing. In 1980, I was dancing with Loose Bruce. My main partner was Kool Keith (Ultra Magnetic MC's), Jesse, and this kid by the name of Yogi, they were lockers. Our crew's name was the Shack Crew. We didn't have any breakdancers. My thing was the Electric Boogie. As a matter fact, we got chased out of Skate Key in the Bronx after we won a contest against Rock Steady Crew. They really were breakers. None of us could touch Crazy Legs because we didn't know how to break.

Push: **So why did you get chased out of the Bronx?**

Supreme: They were the home team, you know how it is. We would also dance with the Force MD's. They were my boys. Stevie D used to pick me up and take me to shows. Back then, each MC crew would have dancers that would represent them at Jams. I think The Cold Crush Brothers had Rock Steady Crew and from time to time we would dance for the Fearless Four. Once the dancing got sour I went back to DJing.

Push: **Name a few of the Brooklyn DJs that were around in the 1970's.**

Supreme: Nut Cracker and there was D) Flowers, Master D and Labro. Master D was the man but Labro had the banging sound system out there. Von K and somebody else who used to rock the Brooklyn Armory. Do you remember the Zoo?

Push: **I remember the Zoo. It used to be a club in Brooklyn.**

Supreme: And Cellars-- that's the club that I could hardly get into, the only thing that would get me over was my dancing. If it wasn't for me dancing, I would have never gotten into any of those parties. I'm going back and forward right now...another place that would never let me in was the Disco Fever! To this day I never been in the Fever and I rolled up there with the baddest crews...they never would let me in. Now back to DJing -- I brought a set of BSR's, we used to call them bull shit record players back then. Technics [turntable brand] came out with the SBL1 's way before 1200's. Nobody had money to buy Technics. We used to put sewing needles in the BSR's and make grooves in the record until we put a hole in.

We had to buy records damn near every two to three days. We would go to John's record shop spend a dollar for a 45-- you know what I'm saying [pausing to laugh]? We would spin Chic's "Good Times" and make the record go *Good-Good-Good times all day! It was butter.*

Push: what was your favorite record to play at a block party?

Supreme: "Love Rap", "Heart Beat", "Got To Be Real" and "Mardi Gras" was my main records-- I'll tear that up to this day! The theme from SWAT was cool but I never liked "Impeach The President" and- what's that record?- the beat went something like this: *Doom- Dom-Domp.*

Push: I think that's "Different Strokes."

Supreme: Yeah, that's the record. You had to be fast to catch that break. Now they have break beat albums with extended breaks. See, we didn't have that back then. You could only play the break; if you let the rest of the record play, it would be some shit the people couldn't dance to.

Push: You had to have skills.

Supreme: Yeah, you had to be fast on the cut-- bam- bam- bam! Now, break beats give you everything. They keep the break going for you and the DJ don't have to do as much work. Back then, you had to be on your P's & Q's-- you fuck up and miss the break you were outta there. If you were a DJ you would have a helper who would carry the records for you. You would stack them and he'd pass them to you while you were spinning- like that I Love Lucy candy episode- you had to keep it coming, keep the records coming: *Boom-bap, boom-bap,*
boom-bap. That's why we wouldn't play breaks all the time because after a while you would get tired. Back then, you had to know the name of the record and the artist because certain records were hard to find. DJ's would cover up their records so other DJ's wouldn't know what they were spinning and when you asked another DJ the name of a record he would tell you a lie so you couldn't get the record. The GodFather sound track was a record that was hard to get. It cost $24. I never had it [laughs]. I wanted it bad. Afrika Bambaataa was the only DJ I knew of that had it. I guess all the other DJs said the same thing I said--
"I'm not paying $24 for a damn break." Bambaataa was the beat master. Bambaataa would play something that wasn't even a beat and the crowd would love it. I would listen to him play and say to myself, now...he's just grabbing records, putting them together, and the

"We had to buy records"

people would love it because he's Bambaataa. He could have you grooving and then play something way off the wall sounding like this: yak-yak-yak-yak.

Push: **Name a few of your all time favorite DJs in New York.**

Supreme: Master Don from the Def Committee-- he was better looking at him in person than hearing him on wax. Most DJs were better when you listened to them mix. He would do tricks on the turntables, turning his body all types of ways; Master Don was the man. Charlie Chase was good. He used to make the records sing. Flash was good too. Brooklyn bad was Master D. In this area it was a brother name Terry- matter of fact, he taught me and my brother how to DJ.

Push: **What were some of your favorite party spots?**

Supreme: L.G. (Lafayette Gardens). You want to go to a good block party you go to L.G. ...you might get shot at but you damn sure going to be at a nice block party. Another place to jam was Nostrand Ave. & Gates Ave. The crowd takes up the whole block. Cellars on Waverly Ave. and the Elks' Club had a little something something and then they fell off. The Fort Greene Senior Citizens Center used to have their thing going on. We had our thing going on. I think the best one we had was House of Power "Soul Powers"- until we had our run in. Until this day, I think the music started the riot.

Push: **Why?**

Supreme: Because we had that shit jumping, man. We had that shit JUMPING! I remember I was on the turntables when that riot broke out. That's when Big (the late Biggie Smalls) would be down there people would battle on the mic's. Another good party we used to do was on Myrtle Ave...

Push: **The Warehouse.**

Supreme: I think we only played about one or two times there. That was the bomb place. Gorilla's Den was all right, but it was just too hot and too spooky.

"Bambaataa was the Beat Master"- Supreme

Afrika Bambaataa

"We showed society that we are articulate and
wise, we showed the world in poverty you do have creativity".

DUST

Park Sounds by Shandu 1979

BROOKLYN HAD THE THE DJS
- Chuck D

F.A.
ROCK

Divine 1981

"**Pieces** came out about **1972 or 1973- back in the days** with
Super Kool, Stay High and **Phase 2"- Stan 153**

A B-boy, Tito of The Fearless 4 and Supreme in the 1980's.

That Brooklyn Bullshit

Infinity ½ WOLE

BklynQueen

THAT BROOKLYN BULL SH-T

Infinity, a.k.a. Half Note: Rapper /Ceo of Paper Girls Inc.

Push: When did you start MCing?

Infinity: I started MCing when I was in Junior High School. I was a cheerleader and I used to write cheers. Then from there I went into MCing— writing rhymes, rapping. You know, when you hanging out at the mall rhyming with other kids-- that's about the (Roxanne) Shante era.

Push: **So who were some of the DJ's you remember out here in Brooklyn and some of the Mc's that probably influenced you?**

Infinity: Boosting Kev! His name used to be Peter Parker Spider Man. He used to get up on the turntables and cut with his feet and stuff. He taught me how to back spin and do some cutting on the turntables, and that's good as far as rhyming... then I could switch up on the beats, you know what I'm saying? As far as rappers in Brooklyn, I grew up with Biggie. Me and him went to the same elementary school, but he wasn't a known rapper. When you say "Brooklyn," the only people I can really remember is Stetasonic-- they were the ones that originated the "Brooklyn, Brooklyn." And then you had MC Lyte, she represented for Brooklyn. Now they (Brooklyn! got everybody. From there, I moved to Queens. I used to hang out by the Coliseum.

Push: So you're also a DJ too?

Infinity: Yeah, that's like a hobby thing.

Push: **Do you remember any of the block parties or park jams? I know you might have been pretty young lor the park jams.**

Infinity: In Brooklyn, yeah we use to have regular block parties where they used to cut off the block. I remember when they used to play "Push Push in the Bush" and "Boogie Oogie," we used to roller up and down the block.

Push: What block was that?

Infinity: Cambridge. We used to have the battle of Cambridge "one" and Cambridge "two." St. James one against St. James "two"—that's where Biggie was from-St. James. We used to have lit-

"BROOKLYN PEOPLE STICK TOGETHER"

tle cheer leading battles, it used to be wild. When it got dark out it wasn't hectic. When we got older, they [the rest of the block) just wasn't trying to hear block parties any more, they had a couple of activities going on. As a whole I think Brooklyn grew up a lot. Everybody was young at one time and we B.I.G. & Junior Mafia all grew up-drug dealing, boosting--everybody was into something. One thing about people in Brooklyn, we all went to school, we all tried to do something with our lives, you know what I mean? Brooklyn people stick together more than folks in a lot of other boroughs. Brooklyn people show a lot of love, we stick together and the community is growing. When I was a little girl, every block around me was abandoned. Today, condos are on every block and that's my word...which is good but the consequences of that are if you're not paying a gee (thousand dollars) your ass is out! Brooklyn is worth a lot. A lot of people think Brooklyn is still wild. It's not like that. We made it a home.

*Push:*True... Who are some of your favorite artists in Hip Hop in general?

Infinity: I used to always like Rakim and EPMD-- they came back strong. Especially EPMD- - they came back like *what?* You know who else I used to like was Kool G Rap. A lot of people now try to rhyme about things he used to rhyme about. Now a lot of people talk about why are you rhyming about drugs, this and that"-- Kool G Rap been rhyming about that since1986. So was Steady B and that other cat-Suicide.

Push: Busy Bee?

Infinity: Yeah, cat's been rhyming about that since way back. I respect when people try to do other things than just rhyme: they produce, they write, they sponsor clothes. That's what makes you a rapper like Biggie- how he showed love to Junior Mafia and love to Lil' Kim. Frankly, I was in Virginia, so that just never happened for me, but I'm here now.

"Brownsville"- Supreme Team

120 (H.O.P.) on 42nd Street, New York City 1985.

"I had the chance to know B.I.G. back in the days, before he became the Notorious B.I.G.; when he was Big Chris and he used to come to the parties and set it, and he was the dopest MC back then."- Cool DJ Law

Photo:Dawoud Bey

Sid, Push and DJ Bones "Brothers Going to Work it Out".

"The Bronx, New York, Boogie Down to the fullest!"- Chain 3, The Death Squad

"PUSH 369" Gates Avenue, Brooklyn

"I can think of twenty-five people who are contributors to Hip Hop"- Pete DJ Jones

Slick Rick

PROFESSOR X

Evolution of Style

THE EVOLUTION OF STYLE

The Late Professor X of the X clan & The Black Watch Movement

Push: In your perception, when and where did Hip Hop start?

Professor X: It started with turntables and the two turntables did not start in Brooklyn. The turntables were brought to the light... well, first I can recall and I'm telling my age now.- I can recall going to basement parties in the East Nineties in Brooklyn, where the DJ became a prominent understanding as a collection to what we (Brooklyn)people know as what Disco and the DJ was going to represent. So some of the most popular parties in New York people used lo travel from all over New York - to come into the Nineties to party - with DJ's like Super Goldy and Undertaker Ash. From there sprung this kid who was the biggest of them, who had a partner. His partner's name was Dice and he was called Flowers.

Push: Thank you!

Professor X: And, not only am I about to connect what Hip Hop versus the DJ versus the turntable was, but I'm also going to say graffiti did not start in the Bronx. As a matter of fact, Flowers and Dice was your first all around-the-city tag team.

Push: OK.

Professor X: The first, OK? That popularity in the becoming of that first recognized graffiti artists gave this new popularity to someone who was able to get by the police and not just tag their name but actually do art right. This has also spun a kind of clothing that had happened at this point: graffiti on the jean suit. The jean suit and the East Nineties parties were symbolic, OK? When you went to these parties starting with **Undertaker Ash**, **Flowers** and **Dice**, **Super Goldy** and quite a few other individuals, they had to find bigger arenas because basement parties became a block party at night, and the' police was not going to have it. Then there were ' some of them that decided we should put it in a | bigger room somewhere, and when these little I places in Brooklyn that was like catering places. | These became your premiere disco places, but I then they began lo be not big enough and in the midst of that crowd when one got into the room, I the two turntables were going on. While the pop

-ularity of the DJ was happening, the DJ could not have a good party by him just being the personality because he was the personality. That was the signal of a good party somewhere-- who the DJ was. But, even the DJ knew the followers couldn't understand when he was literally making one record sound like an hour played record, which we know now as the mix right? In the mix one of the great things to happen was... what you had to have, if you were a traveling DJ, you had to have an MC. Someone that would chant the party on and this person would literally make the place bounce with the DJ on one record for 20 to 25 minutes, when no one else could do that: No one could make someone stand up and party as long as these DJ's at the time; which now started to carry on to other boroughs and created their (the borough's) own traveling DJs. I hear people say **Kool Herc**- with all due respect, I think there's a B-boy stamp you can place there. You might have a first indication but the guy coming out of the Bronx who had one point... listen close now- he's going to sound familiar. When the MCs took over, it was called the DJ Battle. These DJ battles were so popular that radio stations began to promote these particular shows. The guy who came out of the Bronx was **Pete DJ Jones**.

Push: **All right!**

Professor X: He and Flowers were always the talk then. It had to be one of the two, but there were other characters. Let me name some of them: there was a guy called **DJ Maboya**. He used to run the parties down there in the Flatbush area of Brooklyn, which you know would be a Caribbean kind of flavor. Now we are getting to the Caribbean. Another one called DJ
Terror. Yes, man I don't want to tell my age [laughs]. Mind you, at one point and I have a theory with that-oh, let me go back to these DJ battles and MCs: Flowers or **Pete DJ Jones** or Maboya or Plummers, they were the first to bring the equipment with them into a club. From the turntable to the speaker to the whole thing; and they used to truck large speakers because those DJs love a lot of bottom. In order to get the equipment there, they had to have them a little crew. Now, strangely enough- now I want you to pay attention to this from
here sprung something else. Let's say when Flowers performed in Manhattan, he
would have 6 or 7 younger people that would help take his equipment there, one of these guys probably would be your MC. The kids that were doing this weren't really trying to get
paid. They wanted to be around the music and there were things they brought to the music.

Push: **Like what?**

Professor X: There used to be dance squads. The breakdancers. I'm here to say I stand up for it and I will definitely stand by it. I hear the Kool Hercs, I hear all that, I will say that **Kool Herc** and them represent the closer touch to understanding of B-boy. There was a
whole thing going on before that— matter of fact, I can recall your Brooklyn promoters from around town. WBLS (radio station) would hire these promoters to do their parties and stuff

like that. There were several little grounds in Brooklyn that became hot spots because DJs would travel through them places, like a place called the Speak Easy on Eastern Parkway which is now the Tropical something or what ever. That was a big spot for the coming of the turntable and the DJ. These dancers, first you thought they were the help, and then the music got hot and shit. And for younger kids who couldn't get into the club any other way, the thing was you'd link up with the DJ, you'd get his equipment in and you could dance all night. So now [there] was a feast on organized dancing. It was what some kids called the **Famous Flames**. I can't remember all the names but I'm going to say why I'm so stern with this reality. Here's where my age starts to peek out again. I used to be in throb with the DJ. We would go to these parties and it was Disco time, and these guys mixed so well people really came to party, right? I had a different kind of thought, because I thought it was cool- you know I rhyme?

Push: Right.

Professor X: I used to sweat them [the DJs]. What throbbed me was Flowers and what he was doing. I would say "damn", I would watch him take a record like "Fly Robin Fly" and the section he would cut, the bass would hit right on time. Cool people would come in the place and try to stay calm, fresh and smelling good. When the sound hit them, they would be all over the place. I was so enthused with that, I made friends with these guys and I would get closer to the turntables, because I had to get up close to see what was going on. Then something that struck me, that didn't strike me until later on, as I was involved in Hip Hop before it got formed. You know what happened? I was close enough to hear the scratch going on in the headphones man, and in order to mix he had to scratch.

Push: You're right.

Professor X: At that time you didn't let them hear the scratch. You scratched to put the record in precision with the other. I was hearing that before everybody else would hear the beat come in, you know. I'm just saying to you there are other places we can look, closer places to look where Hip Hop started.

Push: What about this argument: DJ Flowers was a Disco DJ and he didn't spin Break beats?

Professor X: There were no Break beats then. Listen to what I'm trying to say, there were no Break beats when Flowers was spinning-- don't let them try that shit, kid, that came after. The reason why you're not going to hear that? Most of the people that can tell, ain't going to tell you their age. You know how Hip Hop do you, Hip Hop makes you want to stay young and vibe-- and get arrested for statutory rape in other towns and all that other shit. *She's only 16, but you're 39* and shit.

[Push and Professor X laugh.]

Push: You know I had a discussion with another DJ and the thing was they [the media] divided New York and really bigged up the Bronx as being the pioneers of Hip Hop, when we pretty much were doing it at the same time. What are your thoughts on that?

Professor X: No! I'm saying the Bronx distinguished it. You have to be a baby before you become a child and a child before you're a teenager. So now what I say to you, let's talk about it in its baby form. I can talk about all of the characteristics of the culture that came out of Brooklyn.

Push: What types of characteristics?

Professor X: Brooklyn was sharp. For instance, you have to ask about a trend that was making Lee jeans that actually broke in the denim era that we can't get rid of-- now that started in Brooklyn. You could not be cool if you couldn't get a pair of Lee's. You had distinguished the side of Brooklyn because in Brownsville/East NY (Brooklyn) section they were into Lee's, L-e-e! That shit was big and baggy, when you came into East Flatbush and Bed Stuy they were into Wranglers, you know what I'm saying? This what started in Brooklyn and ended up in the Bronx. I think Flowers and Dice was the first tag on a wall and if anybody can go back they'll tell you that. People were enthralled with them when they would show up to parties with their tags on their jackets. That made them stars, which spurred a lot others that drew on walls. I'm talking about before **the Ex-Vandals** [graffiti crew] era. Then I started to see the Bronx pick up these traits and they began to be a little more daring. They would make their letters, a little more large, whereas the Brooklyn guys were tagging and splitting. Flowers and Dice were moving, the key to them was to do it fast without getting caught, whereas the Bronx made graffiti a little large and the chances of getting caught greater, you know what I mean? I want to tell you something, man, the person that started to make the absolute sense of it [Hip Hop] was the guy who went into a hotel in Brooklyn, that became a welfare hotel, the President Chateau. There used to be a guy coming there on Tuesday nights, we're talking about the time Flowers is packing these places. There used to be rumors of this guy coming in the President Chateau, using these guys, talking about some rhyme thing. That's when I started to see the guys that would come with Flowers and do dances and MCing, they started disappearing. The guy's name who used to come to the President Chateau, a promoter out of nowhere, was Russell Simmons.

Push: What, *the* Russell Simmons?

Professor X: Russell Simmons! This is before rap records. He was there in on the pulse of those same young kids that started disappearing. All those DJ's that had all that popularity and like the Pete D] Jones and all of that, he started to organize that. Now this is around the time that Kool Here started to become something in my ear, OK. A little before that I was hearing of Kool Here but not like the approach that was happening, coming out of the Pres-

LET ME GO BACK TO THESE DJ BATTLES AND MCS: FLOWERS OR PETE DJ JONES OR MABOYA OR PLUMMERS

ident Chateau, from a promoter called Russell Simmons--You know, he came a little later, but the first time I heard of the organization of it [Hip Hop] and the money making part of it before there were rap records. I was hearing through other promoters who were giving Simmons props because they'd seen a lot of young people at his parties.

Push: **So we are talking about before the record "King Tim the 3rd", Fatback?**

Professor X: Sure, please man, I'm trying to tell you I hate to say- it but I was around long enough to hear the scratches that only the D) could hear in his headphones. I heard the scratch leave the headphones to become part of the entertainment, and that's how I knew where I had to be.

Push: **OK, so where did the telephone receiver come into play with the D|, do you remember that? Most people don't remember that era.**

Professor X: Sure, that was poverty kid, strictly poverty. Who needed a headphone? As a matter of fact, it took a long time for the street DJ to pick up a headphone, because headphones made you a nerd. It meant that you weren't raw enough, that you was on some pretty shit. That DJ might have got beat down and robbed, just because he had headphones in his ear, and it was like that.

"I can talk about all of the characteristics of the culture that came out of Brooklyn"- Professor X

Photo: Lolita Standard

Homeless Man sleep in front of Vanguards/Nod Squad Tag on Fulton St.Bklyn,NY 1972. The Vanguards were one of the original Brooklyn Street gangs.

"Brooklyn Hard Rock" - Thirstin Howl 3rd

ILLUSION TO ILL AL SCRATCH

On the Franklin Avenue Shuttle

"No sleep till Brooklyn"- Beastie Boys

A young Lil Kim, friend and Mo (B.S.D.)

The Renegade Dance

THE
RENEGADE DANCE
KING UPROCK
OF THE
DYNASTY ROCKERS

Push: Where are you originally from?

King Uprock: I was born in the Bronx and moved to Brooklyn at the age of five.

Push: What year are we talking about?

King Uprock: You're talking about 1968.

Push: So what was the Brooklyn Hip Hop scene like in the late 1960's and early 1970's?

King Uprock: When I was growing up in Brooklyn, the Hip Hop scene was kind of underground. I saw my older brother spinning a lot of real soul music and a lot of gangsters were getting into
King Uprock member of the Dynasty Rockers

Push: Can you name a few of the gangs at that particular time?

King Uprock: We had the **Crazy Homicides**, the **Devil Rebels**, they had the **Tomahawks** around, they had the **Savage Skulls**, the Dirty Ones- those are the old gangs of Brooklyn in that era.

Push: What part of Brooklyn did you grow up in?

King Uprock: I grew up in Bushwick.

Push: OK, cool, so why don't you tell us, how did the Brooklyn Uprock start to develop? And can you give us a time period?

King Uprock: Well there used to be this park, Knickerbocker Park, and it used to be these guys playing live congas and Latin music. There were these brothers named Rubber Band and Apache, they were gang members. They used to dis each other to the beat of the conga drums. Eventually, they started making the dance to it, and putting more steps to it. They came up with the idea of having gangs dance against each other rather than having fights. The gangs were trying to get into a positive era. From there on as I was growing up, in elementary school, I would see gangsters rocking and I liked it. When I got to junior high school I picked it (Uprocking) up. I met the guys who were doing it and I learned a little more steps from them.

Push: The Rubber Band that you are talking about, is not the same Rubber Band from the Furious Rockers is it?

King Uprock: No that's not him. Matter of fact, the Rubber Band I'm talking about, they shot him after he came up with the concept of the dance with Apache. He used to go to a club called the Starship Enterprise in Manhattan. He used to always win contests and the other gangsters were so jealous of him they shot him!

Push: Wow-- and that was the beginning of the Brooklyn Uprock. So tell us what's1 the difference between uprocking and top rocking.

King Uprock: Top Rocking is the start of the dance B-boys (breakers) do before they do their footwork or something. It's just so they can do a little footwork on the top, so they can work themselves down to the bottom. Up Rocking is a lot of freestyle dancing, it has a lot of burn moves so you can dis your opponent. When you're talking about Up Rocking you're talking about one dance, when you're talking about B-boying that's another dance. A lot of B-boys don't know the difference, they do Up Rocking and B-boying- it doesn't go that way. You Up Rock or you B-boy. The way I see it, people doing the dance from different cities
and countries, its not their fault. It's the people who are fakers who are trying to dance who don't understand it and just do what they want to do because they're on TV, and other people look up to them and say "oh, that's Up Rocking."

Push: Well how can we change this?

King Uprock: The way to change this? The media. The media themselves. Publications are giving the wrong people write-ups, and all these MC's or Rappers, whichever you want to call them, should stop putting fake ni—z in their videos. Let the real McCoys out. The way I see it, it's jealousy. Some brothers just want to be in the camera all the time. They don't want an original brother out there to let them get their props. Like me! I'm 34. I have to go out there and burn Rock Steady Crew, Kwik Step crew and other crews. These guys don't know nothing about Up Rocking. I mean how can you be in front of the camera doing a dance and then not want to battle me? I'm an originator, I made a lot of new steps into the dance. We had guys from the Dynasty like the legendary Danny Boy who is still dancing, Lil' Dave, Jr. from the Dynamic Spinners...you know these brothers still dance and we can't get no light because B-boys think they can do anything they want, and they won't even hook up an original brother. In 1973 we went see a Karate movie. It was Dynasty something...we used the name Dynasty Rappers. We were one of the original Brooklyn crews.

Push: Can you name a few crews that was dancing at that time?

King Uprock: Oh yeah, we had Touch of Rock, *Phaser Rockers*, *Nasty Rockers*, *The Mysterious Rockers*, *Fast Rockers*, *The Incredible Rockers*, *Explosive Rockers*, One on One,

Brooklyn Rockers, Born to Rock, Born to Burn, Rock with Class, Rock with Style. It's even more than that—there were so many big crews.

Push: Are these all New York Crews?

King Up Rock: All Brooklyn crews from Bushwick.

Push: That's a lot of groups.

King Up Rock: And I have more, you know. I can tell you one thing-nobody gives any credit to the DJ. As an Up Rocker I'm a DJ myself from back in the days. I look up to the other brothers like Disco Stompers, Electifying Sounds, The Disco Twins and Divine Sounds, the crew that sings "What People Do For Money." Back in the days, crews used to battle for equipment, you know what I'm saying? Me and this guy named Caesar were the first little Puerto Ricans to learn how to scratch. We had our equipment and the bigger guys had theirs. We used to play parties and stuff like that. Nobody gives me credit as an old school DJ. I've been DJing way before these other DJs that are now making records, and nobody
gives me my props.

Push: What was your DJing name?

King Up Rock: I used to call myself DJ Mott, Master of Turntables. I was the first Puerto Rican out in Bushwick. Me and Caesar, we were eating up a lot of brothers on the turntable. I said we used to battle for equipment. Eventually we kept getting better equipment--we represented! We used to do the Hustle dance. A lot of Up Rockers used to be good Hustlers too. The reason you wanted to be number one was for the girls because if you was a good Up Rocker, you had all the girls. We never figured Up rocking would go commercial and make a lot of money like B-boying did. So the Bronx, I guess Kool Herc and those guys, made Hip Hop commercial and that's why everybody looks up to them. They took it to the next level but in reality we were doing our own thing. We never went to the Bronx back in those days, the Bronx didn't come to Brooklyn. They figured they might get beat up. We did our own thing and they did theirs. But, to say Hip Hop started there is hard to believe because there's a lot of brothers older than some of the guys that lived in the Bronx, and these guys were all doing hip hop. We had drum machines and stuff like that back in the days.

Push: What would you say to people around the world who believe Hip Hop started in the Bronx, rather than in New York in general?

King Up Rock: Well, I would tell them that maybe they should go into history and find guys like myself. You have to listen to a lot of people, you just can't listen to one borough. You have to see what other boroughs are doing, because we have records that sometimes caught on and the Bronx doesn't even know what those records are. And we used to make plates. They used to have this thing called Sunshine where if you had a tape, you could make it into a record. It used to be called Sunshine. It used to be, I think, out on 48th street. I've-talked to a lot of brothers; I've said, listen, you're from back in the days, you know this record, and if I mention Sunshine, they don't even know what I'm talking about. They don't even know the clubs I'm talking about. You know, people figure I'm 40 years old, I'm from back then. You could have been from back then, could be 40 years old and not even have lived in Brooklyn. So by knowing the music, knowing the dances, knowing the people and the people can speak up for you, that's how you know who's who. A lot of brothers say, yeah, I Uprock and used to live in Brooklyn, and they never lived in Brooklyn, you know? So, that's why people like me, they know who I am. They know me from a shorty and stuff.

I knew all the gangsters and stuff back in the days. I lived right in the middle of everything.

Push: Can you name a couple of the hot spots back then- you know, the party spots?

King Up Rock: We used to go to this church. They used to rent it out, and they had a guy named Crazy Rob. He used to throw a lot of Hip Hop jams and we used to have a lot of Up Rock contests. And then we had them at his place called Yellow Sunshine. It was on Bushwick Avenue. And there was this other place called 110. It was also in Brooklyn, and then we had a place on Myrtle Avenue. It was like a hall. All the halls and the centers we used to rent out, and then a lot of times, we used to DJ in the park. You know, like Bushwick Park, 116th park, Central Park. So it's a lot of parks we used to DJ in and we used to battle outside. And the D)s I mentioned, they're still out there doing this thing, you know? And I spoke to some of them, and we're trying to do a write-up on them. One day, if you want, I could have them come out there, and you speak to these brothers. I mean, you could see what they'll tell you about the Hip Hop. Stuff you've never even heard of.

Push: Lets get into B-Boying. When did B-boying come about? What is B-boying?

King Uprock: B-boying is a dance where you do a lot of footwork and you do a lot of spinning and stuff like that, which people have commercialized. It's called Breakdancing, but the real term is B-boying. I guess speaking to a lot of brothers, meeting them, I've found that most of it came out of the Bronx. Like a guy named Spike, the man with a thousand moves- I talked to him the other day- and, a guy named Fast Break- you know, he's the originator of B-boying and Track 2, you know those guys right there I first mentioned- are from back in the days. They're like the originators of Breakdancing. I spoke to them. I got into B-boying like in the 80's, 1979 to 1980, because I learned from this guy who was in the FMD's (Floor Master Dancers)-- Kick. He wanted to learn how to Uprock so I started teaching him and he taught me a little B-boying, and then I went to Cooper Park in Brooklyn. I met these brothers, Dr. Love and Master Mind, and they started teaching me a little more and then I got down with them. I started dancing and taking people out because I got good in months at Up Rocking. A lot of B-boying steps came out of Up Rocking.

Push: So Uprocking is the mother of B-boying.

King Uprock: A lot of people don't know that, after a while I became a Dynamic Rocker and then an Incredible Breaker with Chino, Brain And Float. One guy could take a whole crew and nobody mentions them as B-Boying, and I be with these brothers. Kid Freeze, another brother from Dynamic, who invented headspins and magnetic glides and tracks, and nobody gives him props! I practice with him because he have some new moves. These are the brothers, we have to get together, I have them all with me. I'll unite the Bronx with Queens with Brooklyn because I figure it's not one man, it's a bunch of us and that is what's going to show love.

"THE GANGS WERE TRYING TO GET INTO A POSITIVE ERA"

Push doing Head spins at The New Muse.

"A lot of B-boying came out of up rocking"
- King UpRock

Rockafella starts the battle with Break Easy, Mr. Loose, Alien Ness

"Danger" - Blahzay-Blahzay

EASTERN PARKWAY PARADE, BROOKLYN, NY 1983

Next Generation

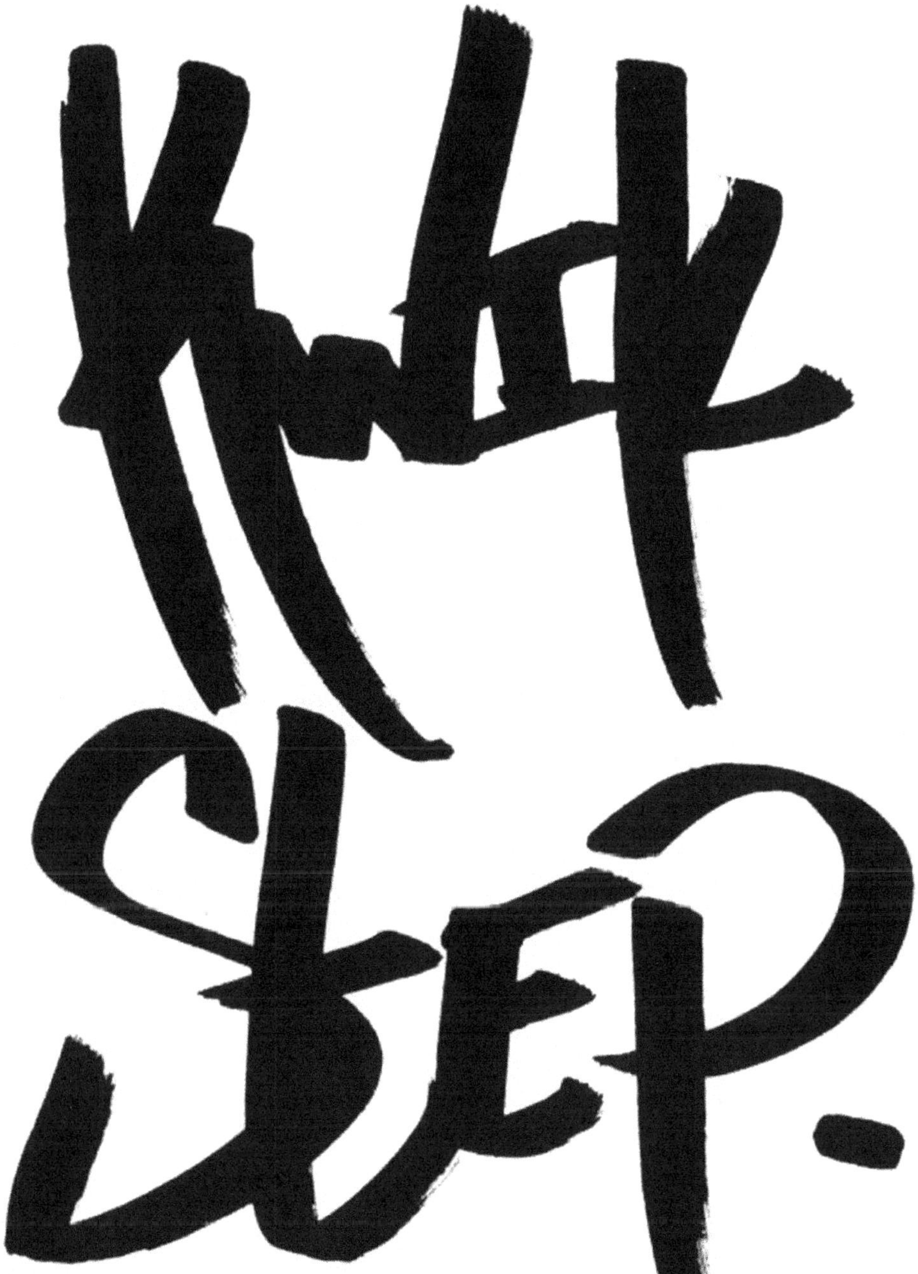

KWIKSTEP OF FULL CIRCLE

Push: Ok, the tape is running.

Kwik Step: OK a lot of brothers, they say you wasn't there in 1978, around my way. You didn't experience what I experienced, and all that is good, but you know what? When Rhythm Technicians came about in '86, '87, '88 you weren't there either. You know what I'm saying? When we were keeping it real, when it [breaking] was totally dead, we were going all over the United States, so I can say you wasn't there either. Where were you? But, you know what? We don't need to say that because you made an effort in those time eras, and when you stopped, it was all good. If it wasn't for you, a lot of people wouldn't be inspired but if it wasn't for Rhythm Technicians and Ghetto Original, a lot of people wouldn't be inspired from '87 to '88 on, all over the United States, and realize that this is a cultural expression that needs to be preserved. So you know what? It's a group effort- it's not up to any one group, do you know what I mean? Or, individual. It's up to the whole Hip Hop community, which comes from an urban influence.

"I was one of
the only people
locking and
doing the robot
in High School
in 1973"
- Shock "a" Lock

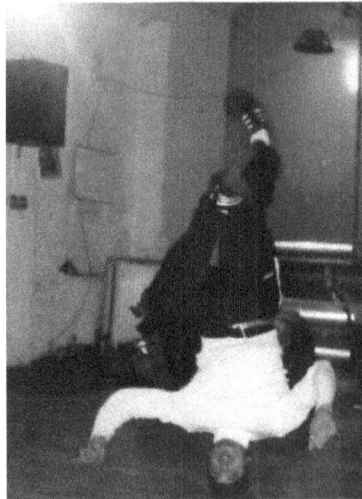

The Wrath of Tron

TRON

THE WRATH OF TRON

TRON: POP LOCKER AND ARTIST-RAW VERSION

Push: What borough are you from?

Tron: BROOKLYN! BROOKLYN! The B to the K to the L to the Y to the N.

Push: How did you receive your name?

Tron: When I first started dancing, I had a partner. There was two of us and what not. I was trying to figure out a name, but the only thing I could think of, was to look through the dictionary and everything-- and it had to sound mechanical. I didn't want it to sound corny, so it was like-"electron" sounds cool and it was two of us. I was Electron 1 and there was Electron 2. After that, my man decided to stop dancing. I was teaching him. He wasn't into it too much, so I just kept Electron but then it was like, that was wack. I wanted to cut it short, so I just took the "elec" off and then "Tron", that sounded cool-- it was off to me, but it was chill. Plus, my first name starts with a T so it was all right, and then the movie came out. So that was it, and it stayed like that ever since.

Push: When did you start dancing?

Tron: 1982, when I went to Art and Design (high school), I started dancing. I got into dancing and that was from a female group. I forgot the name of them. There was a talent show and the girls was performing there- it was three of them, Vanessa, Deirdre and Paula- and they ripped shit. They ripped shit! I was like, this dance is phat. Then I seen Fable and Wiggles talking to them. You know, I was a freshman then. I seen Wiggles and them showing them shit or w whatever, that was the next day after their show . I saw Wiggles and Fable- them motherfuckers even made me- I was like S-H-I-T, what the fuck? I have to learn that dance right there! I had to learn that dance and that was it, ni---z. I was not having it.

Push: Why don't you name the group you came out of?

Tron: I started the Breakdance group The Circuit Breakers, and when it came down to Hip Hop dancing, I had the J.C. Dancers opening up the shows at Union Square (club)-- all the shows before the rappers came out and everything.

Push: Name some of the groups that were giving you problems as a breaker.
Tron: To tell you the truth, I didn't really have any problems with groups dancing if you're saying Breakdancing.

Push: Pop Locking.
Tron: Breakdancing, I didn't even battle too many groups. I roasted a lot of ni---z along with other motherfuckers who were nice like Stretch and Powerful and Illusion, with the J.C. Dancers in Hip Hop, I.O.U. Dancers and anybody else who thought they were nice- word! Fuck that Scoop and Scrap (Big Daddy Kane's dancers) and them ni---z, you know I'd given them all love though, ni---z knew what time is was- word 'em up!

Push: So who was your Pop Locking competitor? The worst?
Tron: There was only one guy out in Coney Island where I lived at, the one who did the Mtume video. His name was Danny Blake. He was nice, he just had a lot of crowd, he lived out there and people knew him. He was nice, though, and plus he had the video behind him. Then I was dancing, but nobody really knew it. I was the Brooklyn kid hanging out uptown and in the Bronx. People really didn't know me. Every time they would mention his name, they would mention my name and every time they mentioned my name they would mention his name; so it was like those two got to get together and that was it. He got dusted off too, in the end, he got it. W e did our little battles and everybody was on the wave, but it was an ongoing thing about who was the best one out there in Coney Island. He was the only one I could say who gave me a really hard time, and I really wanted to damage him and- you know- gain that respect- and that was just around the neighborhood. Uptown people heard of me when I use to go to the Zulu Nation parties or hang at the P.A.L. They would be like, your name is Tron right? You're from Brooklyn right? That let me know brothers from uptown and ni---z in Manhattan and Harlem and Queens- that let you know you're nice, when ni---z was talking about you at the Latin Quarters, the Roxy.

Push: What were some of the differences between the Brooklyn dancers and the dancers from uptown?
Tron: Well I think...I don't know, to tell you the truth, because I mean I hung with both - I
can't even say the difference. I just hung with nice motherfuckers, I wasn't hanging out with ni---z that was wack! It's as simple as that, everybody just learned from everybody. You understood it wasn't "I'm the best, you're the best," it was like "we nice and all wack motherfuckers get roasted." It was like eating. I like eating wack motherfuckers-- we just went out and ate, you know? I would either be around Rock Steady or LockaTron John and that little kid who

"You need to know we wrecked sh*t and we need to be recognized right about now." - Flin-T.O.P.

Fresh Generation members Animal, Push & Frank Swift at the New Muse Brooklyn, New York.

Art Scott was the original creator and publisher of Fresh Magazine

Push: Normski?
Tron: NORMSKI! Kalima and Mohammed and them ni---z, it was always respect and wasn't like don't be dancing in this circle. If you was wack, they would box you out the circle (Breakdance circle). I always got into it and did my thing and we all did our thing-- it was all about respect. It was all about the acceptance. Rock Steady and The Electric Company- them ni---z was nice, they were on, running with Lady Blue. Lady Blue was taking them overseas and everything. They were setting the forefront for all of that shit. So when they would come to the Roxy or the Funhouse, ni---z would step back and they would get busy, and it's all love; and they're with their other homeboys breakdancing, and they were nice! You would say, oh, that's so and so, that's Freakazoid, and oh all right, ni---z know them. There's respect and I want that respect from them, and then when they started breakdancing and doing shit, you'll hang around, you wouldn't try to burn ni---z; you would come out, dance and have fun with ni---z and what not and rip shit. When they accept you, they say "yo you're nice." Or, when they finish doing their little thing, after you came out and they come out after you, and point to you, you'll say "oh"-- they would want you to come out again, and see how nice the ni---z is- "oh that ni--- is nice." Dancers like to watch other dancers dance. It's as simple as that, like singers like to hear other singers sing. They respect the ability, because you both have...if you want to call it super human power and shit. If a ni--- is wack, get the fuck up out of here, you're garbage, you can't even hang in the circle they'll be "all right-all right" and he's done. That's how the shit used to be.

Push: Why don't you name some of the Breakdance crews out in Coney Island?
Tron: There wasn't any real Breakdance crews out in Coney Island, that shit was the boondocks, me and Danny Blake. Who else? Him, my man Junebug, he was down with the GMC's, I'm telling you straight up ni-.

Push: let's talk about the Fresh Kids.
Tron: Who the hell was that?

Push: Fresh Kids from Coney Island.
Tron: Who the hell was that?

Push: Bandit.
Tron: Oh the Break dancers, the C.C. Rock, oh them ni---z was, that Bandit...ok Bandit and them ni---z, C.C. Rock, Zance and all them ni---z, them ni---z was nice. Zance-- that ni--- had head spins out of his ass, that's the first ni--- I seen do 50 head spins, head spin continuously, besides Lil' Lep, but Lil' Lep and them used to drill. Crazy Legs could do that shit, the head spins, and keep spinning and spin; Zance used to be able to fucking spin, spin and then slow down and balance himself and spin again without touching the fucking floor with his hands

Push: Sea Rise that's in Coney Island?
Tron: Yeah, Sea Rise in Coney Island yup! That was one of the projects out there. But as far as Pop Lockers out there, I was the only Pop Locker besides Danny Blake. We were the motherfuckers that inspired everybody else to dance or what ever.

Push: So you had it on lock down.
Tron: Yeah, ni---z knew, I used to go home and eat dinner at 6 o'clock, walk my dog and then go eat. My moms wasn't having it. I'd be at the dinner table, ni---z would come to my house banging on my door saying "yo you need to come down the Island because these ni---z is out there roasting everybody" - *Oh word?* So I would eat, say what's up, good bye or whatever, see what my parents needed and break the fuck out, get to the Island and it would be somebody I know like Stretch and them ni---z and I would be laughing, those are my ni---z... so you have no wins anyway. See some ni-- z who is wack like Benji Flex—fuck outta here-- them wack asses. I hated that motherfucker, word 'em up!

Push: You mean Benji Flex from the ABC (Another Bad Creation) Crew?
Tron: Word! I AIN'T GOING TO FRONT- BENJI FLEX W AS NICE! He just was a fucking big headed ni---. Stretch roasted that ni---, it was like a deadlock tie but the crowd liked Benji a little bit. He battled my man Junebug, because I didn't want to battle him. I was like *man fuck him, I'm going to wind up punching him in his face.* Anyway he battled my man Junebug, he did some shit because I was teaching Junebug so that was my pride. It was cool-- my man did his thing, he learned to battle. But Stretch and Benji battled when they had the school break down in Sheep shead Bay down there-Brighton Beach should I say rocked that ni---, right there on the beach. He got rocked-- Stretch rocked him, hell yeah. Stretch is doing mad videos.

Push: Who is Stretch? Why don't you tell everybody about Stretch?
Tron: Yeah well he's cool with me, that's my ni---. Stretch does a lot of choreography work. You seen him do work in Michael Jackson's videos, the W ill Smith shit, "Gettin' Jiggy With It" and a lot of other shit. You know, that's one of the nicest motherfuckers there is out there.

Push: How did you get in to Hip Hop dancing and regular dancing?
Tron: Well with Stretch, I would see him around the clubs, I seen him dance plus he used to dress wild. Shit, he used to stand out. He was wearing baggy shit when ni---z wasn't wearing baggy shit and he had that collegiate look with the Converse and the baggy socks, baggy pants and a long dress shirt. I was cooling with little Swatch watches and shit...all right, all right, that Benetton shit, and Peter Paul, you know what I'm saying? I said all right, that's the format, so I learned how to dress besides the Breakdancing, you see. I went from

"We're taking it to the next step and we're taking our time doing that, because we learned from the past...if you rush through things and you're not thorough about what you do, you pay the consequences."- Popmaster Fable

Speedy E of The Fresh Generation.

I went from two separate eras, from the fucking Breakdancing to the New Jack Swing shit. Half of these moves ni---z is doing now out here is moves that ni---z were doing way back. I sit back and say ah I remember us doing that-- like Kid 'n' Play with their little two step foot clap shit. I remember when we first did that shit at Union Square and then see these ni---z doing the shit in a video-- get the fuck outta here, these biting ass ni---z. "Do it my way" [Tron sings] --you biting asses! I'll tell you who used to be wack-- Leg 1 and Leg 2 [laughs], MC Lyte's dancers-- them ni---z was wack. I couldn't believe they got a job dancing. The nicest ni --z I seen dancing after I stopped dancing was Kool G Rap's Polo dancers. I liked the way they danced. They were smooth too, dancing in the Streets of New York video. Scoop and Scrap were cool too but too corny; they tried to be smooth.

I had my own group, The Circuit Breakers, so I was doing a lot of shit like that. Mainly, I was a solo. Most of my posse was school motherfuckers from Art and Design. They weren't the bad boys of Art and Design, ni---z just liked dancing. They weren't hanging out too late. My man Mark Jarvis, he used to live up in the Bronx. Boom-- my man a.k.a. fucking Richard-- I forgot his last name...who else? Hakeem, my man Von, Scott Chester, one of the best motorcycle detailers in the world, and my man Muhammad-- he was cool. It was just ni---z who liked to dance. I was always going to the Bronx. I was always alone when I was in school. Or, maybe if we all would go to the Roxy we were The Circuit Breakers, but otherwise it was just Tron. I was for dolo, just running around trying to do what Rock Steady and the Electric Company-- not to mention the Dynamic Breakers and Glide Master, Wave and New York City Breakers [were doing]. I remember when I roasted Larry Love in Harlem.

Push: Larry Love who used to dance for the Furious 5?
Tron: Yeah, yeah, the one with the record-- gassing him up like that ni--- was nice (singing) "Pop it Larry Pop it"-- get the fuck outta here! He tried to roast me on his record and I roasted him on his own record. On Second Avenue and 123rd Street, where they used to throw parties on the second floor, I roasted him. Then those nl---z tried to shoot us-- I remember that shit, ni---z tried to jump us. You see, they fucked up- because I didn't come out there with those dancing ni---z, I came out there with my posse-- I was the only one dancing.

Push: What type of posse?
Tron: BROOKLYN NI---Z, BROOKLYN NI---Z who ain't fucking having it! W e were the only Brooklyn ni---z [in the club] in Harlem yelling "Brooklyn," yeah, plus ni---z got row dy-- "where all the Brooklyn ni---z at?" W e were in a circle of mad ni---z and ain't give a fuck. Then we got outside the club they tried to swing on us. They got rocked. Ni---z tried to rip ni---z and they were busting caps-- them ni---z got rocked! My people was carrying big shit back then. I don't fucking hang with kids, I hang with grown fucking men. Ni---z were

older than me and I'm 32, so you know the mentality of those motherfuckers, and they already had gats...It's all good. Dancing opened a lot of doors for dancers to see the world and see what they could do besides the regular 9 to 5.

Push: What would you say to all the new Pop Lockers who don't know who you, Fable and Wiggles are?
Tron: You keep doing your thing. W e don't hang out any more so I won't say don't try to dis me because you don't know who the fuck I am in the club-- get your ass rocked [he laughs]. I can still do all that shit, word-- keep doing your thing, keep dancing. Pop Locking and Breakdancing are like martial arts. You have to figure out better ways, more effective ways and combinations, shorter combos to get rid of your opponent quickly; because the whole thing with battling wasn't- you come out- I come out-you come out-I come out- you dis me-I dis you with the mime shit. Nah! That's that corny ass motherfuckers' way. When ni---z is nice, you come out- I come out...and you don't come out no more because I'm going to dance on your ass and combinate on your ass from fucking locking to knee spins to floor combos to popping-- all that shit! I'll dance on you for the whole record and then, you come out with your heart beat and little float- - get the fuck outta here. That's how you come [in a circle]... 1-2-3-4-5 and get out.

Push: What would you say about the circles today? I notice most people in the circles are not that tight.
Tron: They're wack, you're supposed to block ni---z out like that, block him out or get in there while he's dancing...give him a little respect-- half a minute. Half a minute, then start getting wild. What we used to do in circles is not hog the space. It would be two of us dancing-- you do your real phat shit in 4 type moves all flowing into one, and pop your ass out and let the next man get in. Some of them motherfuckers get in [the circle] there and want to be fucking Denny Terrio and they be wack. W e used to make mad circles and ni---z used to want to jump in our circle. Why? When ni---z used to see us dance, they used to say "oh, they're getting amped," and the whole crowd would start looking at us, and then some unknown would come in on flag and dance so that bit--es could sweat him-- like he's down with us-- get the fuck outta here. Wrong! Yo, money beat it. Get up out of here—beat it duke! You got to be nice. If you're nice motherfuckers can't deny you, ni---z player hate you. I've been player hating-- fuck it, we just battle, simple as that. During my whole career, nobody will ever say Tron got roasted-- never-- never! The key is you hang with nice motherfuckers, you sleep it and you eat and breathe that shit. It's like kung fu. Anything you want to do you're constantly doing that. I used to be in my bed asleep at night, dreaming in my brain, thinking about the move. I would wake up and say "oh shit" and try to do it and then go back to sleep. Then the next day, I'd be down in the basement cutting class,---

Breakdancing in gym class which I'd ha v e 4 periods later, and I'm down there bugging out with everybody else. So you have to keep practicing the dance if they're paying you. Right now, dancers don't get that much light. You have to be a choreographer to get the just pay that you should get, because in dancing they look at you-- you're nothing but a fucking prop, even though dancers are making artists look good because people don't want to watch artists on stage. You [rappers/singers] ain't doing nothing special. You're just the old person on the microphone and nothing's going on behind you.   You're on stage waving your hands and your boys walking behind you all right, fine.

It's pleasing to the eye to watch the artist and the dancers. The artist is figuring you're the props that make him look good. He's not going to pay you that much money because dancers are a dime a dozen, just like rappers are a dime a dozen. Ni---z get bullshit deals and ni---z get put on right away. Ni---z get put on the shelf for eight years and ni---z get put on right away. The record companies are looking at the artist. You're a dime, and that's the way the artist is looking at you [the dancer]. "You want what? $150 a show and a perdiem? Nah, I'll give you $50 a show." Mother fuckers be dissing you. You go to video shoots and just dance-- no, I want to be a theme dancer. When that camera pans off of the artist I'm going to be in the next shot. Like when we did the working overtime with Diana Ross, which I had a nice spot in that mother fucker. You see me, I tore shit up for about 5 seconds. They have crowd dancers and theme dancers, the ones who do routines. That's w here you get your light.

T hat's w here you get your dough and other work. Make sure you're being seen if you're going to make videos. That's w h y JC and Stretch were doing so many videos like the girls. I choreographed all of Heavy D's tour with Stretch, Khalif and Link.

RAP KILLED THEM

Rosie Perez...all right, on the first video We Got Our Own Thing (by Heavy D) [Rosie] called me cause she's in Cali don't know -know New York dancers. Don't know no fucking floor moves to fucking help her, alright? T he b--c h ain't give me no fucking credit on the fucking video. And the b--c h still owes me four hundred fucking dollars. Every time I see her I tell her and she knows. And she's from Brooklyn that's what make it fucking worse. W e all grew up as kids in this business, from just hanging out to like-- if you want to say CEO's of record labels-- PUFF Daddy. Ni---z knew Puff w hen he was a dancer, you know w hat I'm saying? Everybody grew up in this industry. **You shouldn't do foul shit to ni—z** you're going to be in the realm around, because believe you me, mother fuckers are going to hold that against you. And don't blow and you doin' foul shit to ni---z and be large, you understand what I'm sayin'? Because those ni---z are going to be your demise and your downfall, 'cause believe you me, mother fuckers gonna get you, alright? Ni---z gonna get you. Alright? Puff Dad-- that's ho w it is, man, sh-t. We know w hat time it is with that les -son, alright? Two mother fuckers is missing off the face of this earth because of that bullshit.

Them two ni---z ain't kill each other, rap killed them ni---z. Alright? I hate to sa y it, man.

-TRON OF THE ALMIGHYTY
CIRCUIT BREAKERS

Future

future

_The Legendary Mix Master **Pete DJ Jones**

The Future
The Legendary Mix Master Pete DJ Jones
Bronx Native
"Pete DJ Jones- Old school"

[Pete DJ Jones reads Jeff Love Interview]

Push: What are you thoughts on Jeff Love's piece?

Pete DJ Jones: The guy who wrote the article. I think he has the right idea. He's right on top of it, everything he is saying is what happened to Hip Hop. It's divided according to groups, crews, boroughs and cities; it's just like gangs. Like he said, it goes back to African roots—it's a cultural thing. Nobody knows where Hip Hop came from but God. Also, no one person can take credit for it, nor can two or three people can take credit for it. Actually, I can think of twenty to twenty-five people who are contributors to Hip Hop. The only persons who can take credit for it are the artists themselves, that put the Hip Hop groove on their records in the mid 1970's.

Push: For the record, Pete, when did you start spinning?

Pete DJ Jones: I started in 1970. I did the first Grambling-Morgan game in Yankee Stadium. I wanted to give a party at the bar near me in the Bronx--everybody was booked, and I couldn't find a DJ. So I called my old friend Rip, from Rip and Cliff, who inspired me to be a DJ, and they couldn't do it, but they said they could help me put a system together. I went down to Sam Ash and I bought me some turntables, some amplifiers and I used their mixer--which was the four knob mixer that you turn one turntable and one down-- and I played my own music. I had a jam packed crowd that night; as a matter of fact, the guy gave me the club every Saturday thereafter. My man Sanders from Three of a Kind Plus One. Do you remember them?

Push: No.

Pete DJ Jones: He gave me the name Pete DJ Jones.

Push: So that's where the name came from.

Pete DJ Jones: That's how the name came about.

Push: The Legendary...

Pete DJ Jones: Pete DJ Jones-Old school! [Pete and Push laugh]

Push: Let's talk about some of your battles with Kool Herc, Flash and some of the other DJs.

Pete DJ Jones: Yeah well, I battled Kool Herc at the Executive Playhouse or Sparkle or what ever it was called. I heard of Kool Herc playing, but I never seen Kool Herc play. I battled Clark Kent.

Push: The original Clark Kent?

Pete DJ Jones: Clark Kent, the guy who wears the glasses. He played the music for Herc. I never seen Herc rap or play music. I'm not even sure if he's trying to cut me out of Hip Hop; I'm trying to see where he fits in Hip Hop. I know he played the Incredible Bongo Band, but I'm not even sure if he was the first guy to play that. So I don't know Herc, man, let's get it together. Everybody is a contributor here.

NOTE: *Pete DJ Jones acknowledges Kool Herc's contribution to the culture of Hip Hop, however he states it was many DJ's which contributed to the foundation of Hip Hop.*

WANTED

KEN WEBB

PETE D.J. JONES

DESCRIPTION
HEIGHT: 6'0" WEIGHT: 165 lbs.
BE ON GUARD FOR: Unusual loud mouth and has tendencies of talking a lot and incessantly — You'll hate him in the mornings.
· LAST HEARD: On radio station WBLS this morning.

LAST SEEN: M.C. at Bohannon Concert
IDENTIFYING MARKS: Small ½ inch scar on left cheek — Also likes to see people having a good boogie down time! Likes to mingle with the crowd — he's a very shifty dude — we extreme caution upon approach him.

DESCRIPTION
HEIGHT: 6'8" WEIGHT: 230 lbs.
BE ON GUARD: For very heavy stereo equipment he lugs around. Armed with over 2,000 watts of disco power, and should be considered dangerous — dance on site of him.
LAST HEARD: At Adrians disco, The Pub, Jimmys, Pippins, Riis Beach.
LAST SEEN: With female accomplice known only as "Becky".
IDENTIFYING MARKS: Mole on left theigh and extreme height. Also likes to play non-stop boogie music

ALIVE & PLAYING SAT. OCT. 5

THE FACTORY

94-21 Merrick Blvd.
Jamaica, Queens
On Merrick Blvd. between Archer & Liberty

FREE GRUB
(Chicken & Rice)

EXTRA
A Special Presentation will be made
to the "Women of Distinction of Queens"

$4.00
10-4 A.M.

SHOWDOWN DISCO FUN

KEN "SPIDER" WEBB & PETE D.J. JONES WILL BE TOGETHER
WITH 3,000 WATTS
OF DISCO SOUND POWER

"WE LOST 2PAC TO VIOLENCE, WHY KEEP IT GOING?" -B.I.G.

Note
Norwood Jennifer,"Jamz",Hits March 17,1997

Top Talent In Action

No. 1
PETE "D.J." JONES

Action **Disco**

OVER 21 ONLY!

Friday, March 18, 1977

10 pm - 4 am

"What Hip Hop really means? The only thing I'm going to tell you, it is the most multicultural, multiracial, age breaking music ever produced" - DJ Marc B

Dev Large aka DJ Super Kon, Friend & Push at a Brooklyn House party in the 1990's.

"We show up, to grow up"- Fast Break

Kwik Step at 88Hip Hop.

R.i.p.

Rerun (What's Happening) aka Penguin was a original member of Don Campbell's Lockers.

"Brooklyn"- MC Lyte

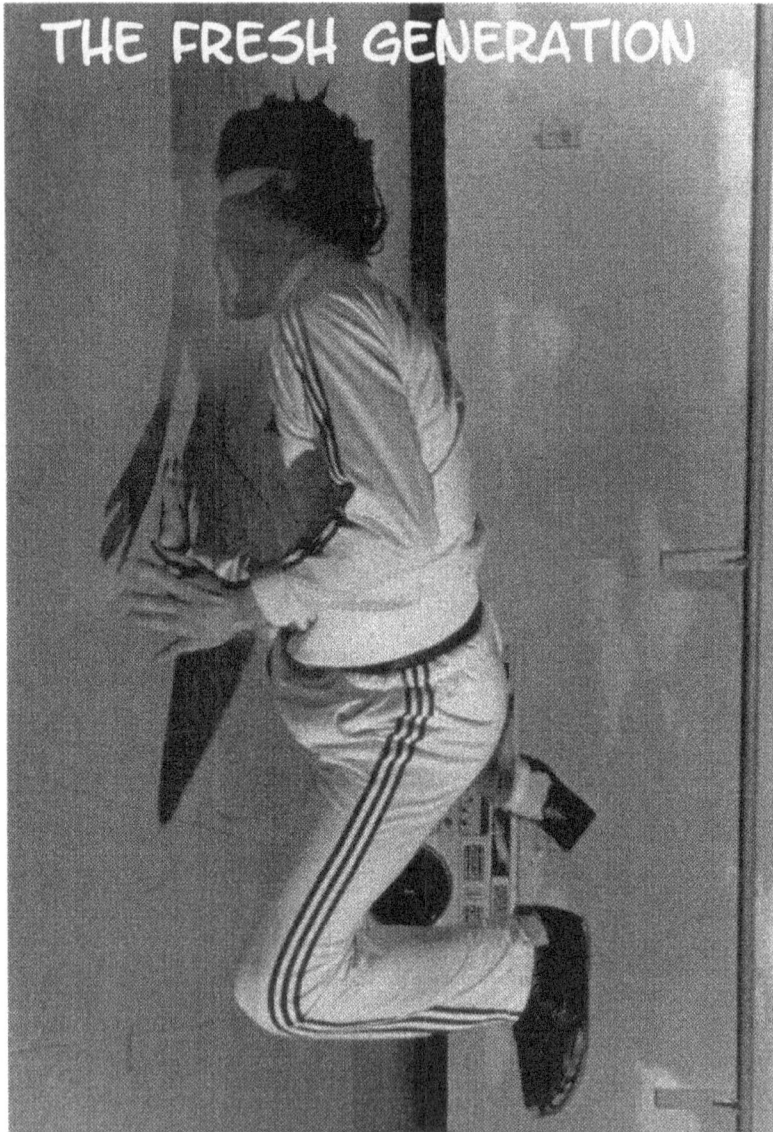

Frank Swift Rocking Floats.

"Do or Die Bed Stuy"- Divine Sounds

BROOKLYN
HARD ROCKS

Respect

TONY

PATRICK

RESPECT

Tony Patrick, former Editor of Word Up magazine

Push: My question to you-- with all the elements in Hip Hop, positive as well as negative-- how can we preserve Hip Hop as an art form?

Tony Patrick: It's really just going to have to go back to the Underground.

Push: Why?

Tony Patrick: It has to go back to the Underground because right now the people who are in control of it are on the industry level. It's a multi- million dollar business. These folks are not concerned with preserving the art form, they just want to see what they can recoup on their returns. When I say recoup, I mean how much money can they make out of it. All the artists are basically being used and they're allowing themselves to be used. I mean-- for example, Lauryn Hill is the only one singing about consciousness in the industry. If you look at an artist- God bless the dead- Biggie, he never said nothing about making improvements in the community, at all-- nothing. If you listen to the majority of his songs, it's drugs and gun play. You listen to Biggie and Puffy's songs, it's being jiggy and gun play. Another element of Hip Hop that needs to be preserved is-- just giving the respect to the old timers because with out them there wouldn't even be Hip Hop. A lot of artists you hear today, there are some that give respect to the old timers but the majority of them, they don't really care about that one way or another. It's gotten to be such a state now, that the only thing I can advise an artist is make your money while you can and just get out and try to form a business of your own. And don't try to make it a lengthy career because it's not going to be that way.

Push: You mean rapping, right?

Tony Patrick: Exactly.

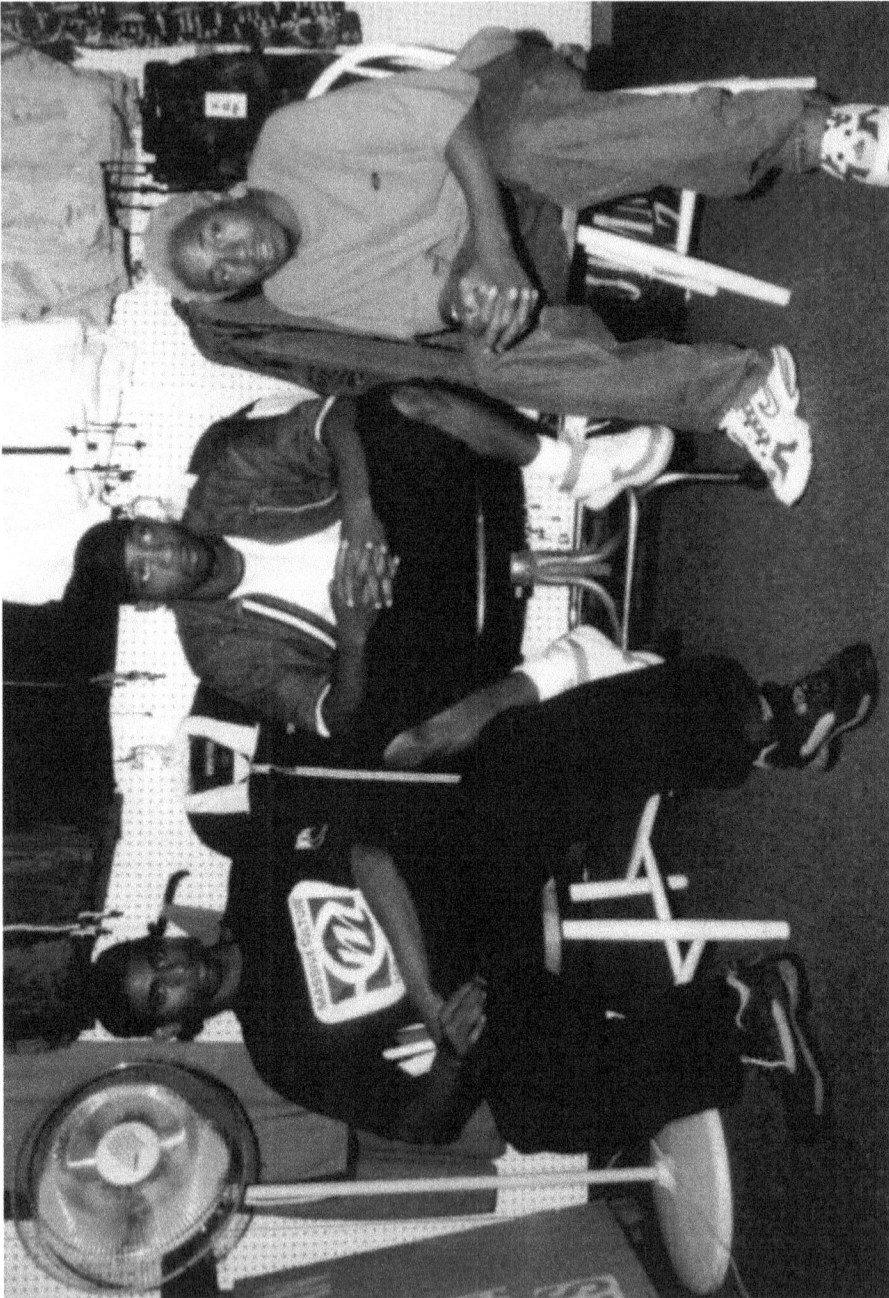

Stress, B.I.G's Junior Mafia's Chic Delevic, a member of the original Brooklyn Street Dancers

Hip Hop is not a sound

CosMo

Strafe & Cosmo

HIP HOP
IS NOT A
SOUND
COSMO OF
NEWCLEUS

Cosmo B: Hip Hop is what they are calling it now, but you got to remember when this whole thing was formed, we didn't have a name for it. We were rocking the crowd and if you want to call what has now evolved into Hip Hop "Hip Hop," then you got to call the collective stuff like "We Will Rock You" Hip Hop. Because as a fellow battle DJ to a fellow battle DJ, that's what you put on when you was telling the sucker down there "we are about to take you out sucker." Obscure Disco records like "Bite Your Granny," that was Hip Hop. Records that some people might call Disco was the classic records, probably one of the most important besides "Good Times" to Hip Hop, of all times, was "Love Is the Message." That's Hip Hop. Hip Hop is not a sound. It's a movement. And what it was, it was a rebellion in the early 1970's—when we went out in the street and said "yo, this is what we're doing, we don't care about nothing- we're going to have a good time. All the cops, we don't care what they say, we don't care about the clubs the DJ's. Yo, we ain't about making no money. We're about rocking this crowd." And, just about any day in the summer time you could have about three, four thousand people in the park, rocking to three or four D)'s battling. It wasn't about shooting or killing, it was about a good time. That's what Hip Hop is.

BROOKLYN EDUCATION FACT
Public education began in Brooklyn when the Common School
System was organized on May 6, 1816. This date also marked the beginning of school segregation. Blacks were taught in Brooklyn's first district school in segregated quarters. Later William M. Read was hired as the first Black teacher. However, in 1827 Blacks were cast out of the district school for unknown reasons. To overcome this reversal Henry C. Thompson and others erected an African Free School on Nassau Street. George Hogarth became its most outstanding principal in 1830, officiating until 1841. -**An Introduction to The Blacks Contribution to Brooklyn**

TO:PUSH

The Raw Un Cut Presents:

JAMES and the TOP Crew

IN HONOR OF DONDI

"Hip Hop started in all 5 Boros"
                    -Grandmaster Dee

W
H
O
D
I
N
I

The group consisted of rappers Jalil Hutchins and John "Ecstasy" Fletcher, adding legendary DJ Drew "Grandmaster Dee" Carter.

NOTE: Brooklyn had DJ Master D & Grandmaster Dee

Jamestop Graffiti Scorch-79 Wett ers Bete.

"Real people stepping to their business and this is how we get down"

Graffiti writers: Jamestop, Scotch79, and Bete.

Push: Let's take it back to BK.

Jamestop: Try and keep this strictly BK.

Push: Jamestop, let's start with you. What was the Brooklyn scene like back in the seventies?

Jamestop: Whew man. First of all, I do have to say back in the seventies, IND's, IRT's too don't even try to front, total domination BK definitely had the IND's down pat, ok. My man Bete is here to represent that. Me from the mid-seventies to about 1978 allright, then from there we passed it on to Dondi and Duro-but fake no jacks son-- T.O.P. dominated like no other crew dominated before. Total destruction, the hell with the law--ok, keep it real! Y'all n---z knew that y'all wanted to get down with the real deal. Real people stepping to their business, and this is how we get down.

Push: What is T.O.P., for the record?

Jamestop: T.O.P. stands for **"The Odd Partners"**, but it stands for a whole lot of other things. You know what I'm saying? So deep, and if you want to talk to me, we can get deep about this whole game right here because I was there. From the point where we dominated-ok--the IND's, the BMT's until we left it off to people like Duro and Dondi, and now we have a third and fourth generation with people like Snatch, Doms and Optict, 2Nice. We just got nothing but the bomb squad. We have nothing but love all the way around New York City right now, and I'm so happy everybody is coming out representing T.O.P. and the love that we have. This brother right here is related to me- you see we have the blood going through our veins as far as graffiti is concerned. We're family. A lot of people try to hide the truth of what the truth is--this is my brother though he has white skin and I'm black. I'm a big fan of his because he was holding it down, him and his man Ko, and AC and them doing it Brooklyn style the way it was supposed to be. I 'm just so happy to get the opportunity to speak to you, talk to his brother

"Total destruction, the hell with the law"- James Top

and to be working with this brother right here

Push: Scotch79.

Bete: This is Bete N.Y.C./T.B.K. to emphasize what Jamestop said. When I started writing , this guy was already king. I looked up to him, James, Hulk, Ups 2, Naco these guys were like Top, UE, Spear, Flatbush, DS3, these guys are top man. T.B.I.: The Bush Incorporated.
Jamestop: We used to take all lines.
Bete: And that was in 1975. By 1977 I started hitting trains. First layup was Ocean Parkway-right from there I went off. I started to king the Double R's, the N's and the B's, and I had much respect for the guys that hit the D's, QB's trains. I'm still hitting today. I love writing graffiti. And I'll never stop, and graffiti never dies. Let's turn it over to the new school and let them represent and follow the history, because things like this keep the history alive and make people aware who used to write who and was king, and who gets that respect.

Push: Nice looking out Bete, let's pass it to Scotch.

Scotch79: So what are we talking about Brooklyn?

Push: Let's talk about Brooklyn. What was going on in Brooklyn?

Scotch79: When I came up in Brooklyn, I lived in Gowanus and back then I'm talking about before the blackout-Cats were outlaws. The cats that got me into writing was outlaws with cut-off denim jackets, mc boots, chains, the whole nine-outlaws F.M.D crew. My man CP3, Crazy Pete lived on my block and inspired me. Other cats in my neighborhood was the N.C.B. crew, Roto, Scar, Roto's brother Snak and in Redhook you had the N.S.A. (Non-Stop Action) crew Action, Deal and his brother Buster, Nell and Sun. These kids were doing damage. All the F.M.D's had my Neighborhood on lock EL, Bell. The Fella's these were straight up outlaw crews, yo!

Push: What year is this--1970, what?

Scotch79: Before the blackout. Yo what year was the blackout? (Scotch turns to Jamestop and Bete)
Bete: 1977 man!
Scotch79: Yeah! B.A.D. crew was definitely rep-ing in my neighborhood, my man, Lye 189, Ink 76, he had my neighborhood on lock and these are the cats that inspired me, you know. Long before I ever knew about the IRT's, I was looking at the letter lines. TheT.O.P. crew came with the two-letter names and that changed the whole game because cats like In and To was doing the throw-ups and no one could keep up. You had a kid that wrote- Ike out of Queens-- he had to change his name to Iz to keep up. Iz the Wiz did damage. After that everyone changed to a two-letter name because that was the only way to keep up. Brooklyn was about throw-ups, killing it throw-ups and insides- just killing it.

Push: Where do you see graff going now?

Scotch79: It ain't going nowhere- It ain't going nowhere, here to stay, always has been and always will be.

Push: You represent the Xmen as well?

Scotch79: Most definitely. I got down with Xmen through Tattoo, Raze and Soe. The Xmen was more than just a writing crew. That was a lifestyle, you know what I mean?
Jamestop: No doubt, social phenomena.
Scotch79: The Xmen's parties used to be off the hook! They even had their own brand of dust [angel dust] they manufactured, and stamped it "Double Vision." Xmen was a livelihood, yo. There were MC's, DJ's and breakers. We had a whole women's division. I mean, maybe ten percent of the cats in Xmen used to write, and the ones that wrote took it to a next level. For a while, R.T.W., they had the lines on lock- when they started slowing down Xmen took all city. I have to give R.T.W. their props. They did damage on all lines, but around 1985 when we came up, we was doing things no one would do. Between Nevins and Atlantic- the tunnel is only this big - they used to lay up at high noon. We would kill it. You could see the cops at Atlantic Avenue on the other side, hear them talking. Nobody had the heart to hit shit like that. We was doing ridiculous stuff. Tess and No, they did the stickers long before cats were doing now. The weak pace bombing, you know. You had so many cats down, I especially want to make sure nobody forgets my man Mizer, my man
Charm locked down doing years on years. They definitely rep for the Xmen and are still rep-ing- wherever they're at. Hold your head up.

Joe's Bed Stuy Barber shop- "We Cut Heads"
a Spike Lee Film 1983

BROOKLYN FACT
1983 Brooklyn Graffiti artist Michael Stewart is killed by New York Transit Police.

"The X-men were more than just a writing crew.'
- Scotch 79

"Stick Em"- Fat Boys

BT Brooklyn kids

James Top

Unity

EX-VANDALS

THE
EXVANDALS

U N I TY Brooklyn- Bronx

: Lazar and Bama

1969 and still going..

Push: How long have you brothers been writing?

Lazar: Since'69, 70.

Push: Really?

Lazar: Yeah, how long you been alive?

Push: Alright [laughing].

Bama: We've been doing this a little while.

Push: What trains?

Lazar: The F train, the 2, the 3, the 4 and 5. Basically, everything that ran through Brooklyn.

Bama: He was in Brooklyn, I was in the Bronx.

Push: Really? In 1960...

Lazar: ...69, I started writing on the trains. There was people out there that was like Tree 127, *Flowers, Dice, Undertaker Ash*.

Push: Not Grandmaster Flowers, was it Flowers?

Bama: Yeah, there was a lot of brothers doing it. There was a unified thing happening in New York and in Philly. And it just blew up.

Push: And in Philly, too?

Lazar: No doubt, no doubt. All our friends and all of them go back to that point.
The guys who used to write over on 126th, *Topcat 126*, that's where he learned, 'cause he used to live in Philly.

Push: (looking at their graff on the wall) Alright, I see the Bronx and Brooklyn love. You know, there's a lot of people battling in these boroughs.

Lazar: Way back when, we lived-we were all like 13, 14-we lived in Brooklyn. These guys lived in the Bronx, and the trains used to come down and we'd see all their tags. So we wondered who the hell these guys were and they were doing the same thing. And a couple of times, different guys got together, and we were like oh, OK, so we just hooked up, and had a good time--became friends.

Push: All unity.

Bama: Yeah, we did the unity thing. There were, you know, a few problems, but it was never a major thing. It was always"yo, you write-Oh!" It was about love.

Push: That's peace.

Bama: So Bama, Lazar, the original Ex-vandals. You hear me? In the house.

Push: The original Ex-vandals.

EX-VANDALS

Bama: Yeah not wannabe Ex- Vandals. The real Ex- Vandals

Lazar: I started the War, and I Started Dead after War.

Bama: Writers are already respected(W.A.R.), and D.e.a.d .- (to Lazar) what did Dead mean?

Lazar: I can't remember. It's been so long.

Bama: But there was Dead, there was a lot of great groups-the last survivors, Vanguards—since its crew day, bust out the old crew.

Push: Alright. The original.

BROOKLYN FACT:

Peter and Benjamin Croger, two brothers,
were founders and trustees of
the High Street A.M.E. Church,
the first Black church in
Brooklyn. In addition to their
involvement in church, Peter Crogerorganized
the BrooklynAfrican Woolman Benevolent Society,
the first school for Blacks,
and the Brooklyn Temperence Society
*for Free People of Color.

-An Introduction To The Black Contribution To The Development of Brooklyn

B.S.D. (RENAMED THE FRESH GENERATION)

Brooklyn Street Dancers- Early 1980's

Mr. Squeeze presents **The Final Show down**

BEAT STREET SQUEEZE!©

SAT. APRIL 22, 1985

108 West 43rd Street New York City
(second level) bet. B'way and 6th Ave.

* Free for ALL LADIES * BET. 7-9PM Only!
* Show Time: 10 PM

FREE **B.SS. membership «cards»**

B.S.S. Pictures of YOU for sale!!

This party shall be Vide...tap...d by... N...g...h...t T...i...m...e...

Male MC's

Monzie D and the Tuff 2 MC's
The N.Y.C's
The Pleasures
The Chosen Few MC's
Dismaster Crew
Grand Slam Klan

Performing Live

3 INVASION doing their NEW HIT

Special Guest **ROXANNE's MAN**

A...we...m...f...f...some...es...q...f...qu...t...

Burnin Ernie Dee
The HOUSE **DJ.**

Female MC's

The Phaze 3 MC's
-vs-
Funky Fresh FEMALES

Dance Contest

Created to Rock
Mt. Footwork & Coco Bklyn Bad Boys
Terrific Kids
Almighty Circuit Breakers

Admission: $8.00
DOORS OPEN at 7 P.M.
$2.00 Off for members
$2.00 Off with this FLYER

Celebrity Guest Judges

The Original Beat Street Squeeze flyer

REALISM

SHOCK A LOCK
ORIGINAL EAST
COAST LOCKER

Push: Shock when did you start locking?

Shock A Lock: Locking? I started in the early seventies- probably about 1971 or 1972, being influenced mostly by some of the dancers on Soul Train. I was impressed by of course Don Cambell Lock, Joe Freeman. They had Soul Train dancers on there like brothers named Scoby Doo, James Phillips—these are the influences from the Soul Train perspective. Prior to dancing and emulating the Soul Train style of dancing, my influences was like James Brown, Marcel Marceau who is the master of mime, which most people do not talk about. The concepts that are in the Electric Boogaloo--there were things that they called ticks, waves freezes all those thing come out of mime. If you really want to get an understanding of the root of some of these things , get yourself some video footage of Marcel Marceau and you will see elements of mime that's incorporated into Electric Boogaloo and Locking. Those are foundations for any kind of dance can use in any form dance.

Push What borough are you from?

Shock A Lock: I'm from Brooklyn born and raised in Brooklyn, I've been locking from 1972 up until now. I was one of the only people locking and doing the robot in High School in 1973. Think about this—I'm in the ninth grade-I didn't even discuss my dancing in elementary school so what ever came after 1975, let's say that was just additional stuff to locking. I had already mastered that whole lock format to the point that in the 1970's, I had already asked myself what would Lockers look like if they were shocked. I started looking at cartoon characters where they would plug them into

SHOCK A LOCK!

electric appliances they'd appear like they were being electrocuted. That concept fascinated me, but then I never saw that done by lockers. It dawned on me that I would practice this technique myself and this how the name Shock A lock came about.

Push: What is the name of your group?
Shock A Lock: At the time I formulated group we called Realism and we had one female
dancer named Robot 2. Alisha John, that's her real name. She was the only female in 1974 doing the robot in the High School of Art and Design-- yes.

Push: It seems like a lot of talented artists came out of Art and Design.

Shock a Lock: And just note the years. We did what they called variety shows. We were the first ones to introduce Locking to Lincoln Center stage. We have the photos. In fact, I have the pictures of me before I even started the group in all the locking gear- striped socks, the whole thing, bow tie, derby from head to toe. Perhaps if you was to do a street dance 102, I'd bring out some of them snapshots. I have pictures of the female I was referring to, Robot 2, in her Locking gear doing the robot. The part in Locking you don't see today is the mime technique, where you have the creation of the glass walls. We did that in **1972**, **73** and **74**. Realism, that's where the concept came from- whatever you do, make it look real. If you're going to pull a rope, it has to look like you're actually pulling it. If you're going to lock yourself in a glass cage, you're going to have to look like a cage is around you. All these images have to be in the peoples' minds as real, at the moment you're doing it. If you're going to do the robot, you should look like a machine, you understand? If you're going to do the robot, you should look a machine, don't look like a man doing the robot, look like a robot trying to be a man. There is no one way of doing the robot. Some people do it like a puppet on a string, some people do it like they are battery operated, some people do it like they are computerized. As for us, we can do all of them.

Push: What is your role as a Locker?

Shock A Lock: Specifically as a Locker, my role is to make sure Locking is ushered into the next millennium and so people can pay attention to the foundation of it, which is creativity. We do not have rules that say you can't move this way. You twist, turn, bounce any which way you choose, as long as it's to the beat. If we have nothing to do with Locking, where I'm concerned is- you got to have soul. It is no Shock A Lock without the soul. James Brown is the Godfather of Soul. I'm functioning like the Godfather of Locking, because Don Cambell Lock is the father— take it or leave it alone.

SHOCK A LOCK IN THE 1970's

"Nobody will ever say Tron got roasted"- Tron

Japan's Engine 9 and Shock A Lock.

Rodney C and Sha Rock of the Funky 4 plus 1 more, Push and DJ E Grand at 88HipHop.

Lynn Love air personality of the EZE show of the mid 1980's.

THE E-Z-E SHOW

ON WNYE 91.5 FM
SUNDAY 11 AM TO 2PM
WED. 3:45 PM TO 5PM
FEATURING THE 91.5 MILITIA
E-Z-E HUGHEY LOVE LIL ACE and
C.L DEVASTATOR
LYNN-LOVE

Flyer by Rac 7

GRAFFITI ARTIST PIONEER
The 707 EXPERIENCE

FLINT 707

Push: When did you start writing?

Flint: Back in the fall of 1971, you can say I started there. I used to doodle in notepads and notebooks; eventually they started turning into black books. All they were was just blank pages-- books with no lines. Basically, I would just write my name and put in characters like Spiderman, Daredevil and the Silver Surfer. I would draw the characters with the name. That turned into an exciting thing for everybody, because everybody used to sit in the class and a say, "oh, shit! how did you do that?" I started tinkling with the name and I came up with the name Flint 707.

PUSH: How did you come up with the name?

Flint: I came up with the name Flint 707 while I was in the street drawing with chalk on the asphalt. You got to remember I was about 13 or 14 years old back then. When we were still playing skelley, and stick ball in the street. I was doing the whole alphabet. When I got to the letter F, I started tinkling with names-- Fly, Flin, Flash. I went to 707 Flint-- I said, "that's a bad name." When I was writing in French Script, I started telling the guys my new name is going to be Flint.

Push: What about the 707?

Flint: There's a lot of meaning behind it, depending on who I talk to. 707 came from this plane, Boeing 707. I used to [build] models when I was a kid. At that time, believe it or not, the 707 was the state-of-the-art airplane. It was the quickest, biggest and coolest plane out. Also at that time, they had James Bond 007, so I couldn't sport no Flint 007-- that shit was corny. Flint 707 was the joint. The name it self represented action, something larger than life. It was just something going through my mind and at the time I took it all for granted. I didn't think [graffiti] was going to blow up the way it did. Flint 707 was going to be something mysterious, what it turned out to be.

Every one hanging out with me liked the name, they liked that shit. It was [a] phase where every-one started to get real hot names too. If he was Arrow he wanted a name like Spear. The names started changing. Guys would get names like Dice, Purple Haze, Spin, Super Strut, Lazer-you talk about some shit.

Push: What neighborhood are we talking about ?
Flint: I'm from Bushwick, Bro. When I grew up in Bushwick there was a diversity there. Bushwick had a lot of different cultures; you had the Blacks, The Puerto Ricans, and the Whites-- mainly Italians. Though we had our differences, we looked through our differences and found common ground. We all found out we were suppressed; and with that, instead of colliding and clashing with each other, we all got together and grew strength on what we had in common. That's how this whole Hip Hop culture developed, man. It evolved around our strength to what we had in common, as opposed to our differences. There were a lot of differences.

Push: Like what?
Flint: The differences would be like: "What's this shit about rice and beans?" "What's with the collard greens?" "What's this shit with fucking lasagna?" Everyone was polarized there for a moment. It all changed because when the shit went down, believe or not, we all came together. We extracted the best of what we were doing and took it to another level. The dancing you were dancing, the Salsa-- "you can't dance Salsa?" "I'm going to dance Disco." "Well, if I can't dance Disco I'm going to free style."

Push: Free style?
Flint: When you were dancing back then, you had "Keep on Trucking", you can't hustle off of "Keep on Trucking" so you free styled. Free style was you just made up your own move sand that's basically where that came from. You just made up moves that had nothing to do with Salsa, Disco or Latin- none of that- the twist-- none of that shit. It was "free style." It was just like the white people do when they go to a Rock concerts, they just throw their hands in the air. W e just had a little more rhythm than they did.

Push: So it's similar to Breaking?
Flint: Breaking is an element that derived from it. It's a derivative of free styling.

Push: Let's talk about the crews you were down with.
Flint: The basic crew I was with-- this small crew I was tagging with, was called Diamonds Incorporated. It came and went. When I stopped writing, the whole crew went out. Then, I was also with the United Graffiti Artists. United Graffiti Artists was the first organization [to get artists] off the streets and off the trains, and put them on canvas and painting gallery walls; and I was part of that organization. We were the best of the best. This is something a lot of people take for granted, a lot of people don't know-- we were the first group to paint

--productions. We called them collectives back then. Collectives was when you got 10 or 15 artists together, throwing down on a big canvas 10 feet tall by 32 [feet] long. Now , to this day, people are doing it and they don't know why they are doing it. They called them productions. They're calling each other up, "yo, where are you going? Meet me on the corner of Fourth Avenue and 35th Street. There is big wall there, and we're going to have a production." In essence, basically that's what we did 25 plus years ago. W e were doing collectives.

Push: So what you are really saying is U.G.A. and yourself were the first graffiti writers to hit the galleries.
Flint: We were the first, there was nothing before us. We had an article in Newsweek magazine which was the article that started it all. That was the article.

Push: What year was this again?
Flint: That was 1973.

Push: Pioneers.
Flint: Pioneers and we didn't know it. We were just having fun, man. You know, basically we were just having fun, that's all. Just having fun and having a good time, and it was keeping us out of trouble. It was a lot of other things we could've done, that we could have got into and that would've done us, got us locked up in jail or got us killed. Who knows where we would have been if we would have took that other fork in the road. That's what life is all about-- it's about crossroads you have to make a decision.

Push: When did you stop writing?
Flint: I never did stop writing, but I did stop writing on the walls. My writing continued through the last twenty years. I always expressed my art form on canvas and galleries, because I felt that was the direction it was going and that was the more positive end to it. Of course, I always had people to call me up with walls to paint on, because they like to see the art work. They like to see the expression, they like to see the execution of the work and what it looks like. It's always something different and something unpredictable. It's not anything planned or thought out like the stuff they do now . It's all thought out for weeks and weeks and then they go "wow ." Back then, you just put whatever was on your mind. You had the paint and the time, and you burst out with all this energy and threw up all you had. I never stopped.

Push: What about the trains, did you hit any trains back then?
Flint: I was hitting trains massively. I was one of the first to do the 3D and top to bottoms and all that mad shit. I was on the J train, the M, the RR, it was the QJ, it was the A, the 7's the number 7's because I was selective about the [trains] I went in.

Push: Why?

Flint: Because you didn't want one train next to the other; you wanted one here, one on the other side of town, one uptown and one in the Bronx-- you got your money's worth. Because if you got busted [laughs]...shit but that's the way I was. I used to select the express lines all the way uptown and that's how I chose them. The funniest thing about it-- depending in the type of train, they would switch them over from the BMT's to IRT's so I would paint something here in Brooklyn and then two or three months later, they would see it up in the Bronx and go "oh shit, did you see that?" That's the type of shit I painted back then. I was a visionary because I was doing shit people couldn't even think of! They wasn't even doing it in the books. I was just doing it on the trains, just like [snaps his fingers] this, *Fuck it I'm going to do it like this today*. Another reason why I painted a lot of trains is because I used to swipe a lot of paint. Steal a lot of paint. And I was good at that shit. I used to break it down to ten to fifteen cans at a time, and when somebody was getting caught I was walking out the store the other way. Ten to fifteen cans-- you can do a lot of damage.

FLINT 707!

"Warning" by W.O.P. – Classon Avenue, Brooklyn, NY

Flirt 707

METALLURGY

THE LOST SCIENCE

39 2nd Ave@2nd St,NYC

MAY 15, 1999

An exhibit of works in spray enamels on metal by New York subway legends:

KEL1ST, STAN153, PART ONE, CHAIN3D, SCOTCH79, WEST ONE, DOC TC5, SOE X-MEN, RAZE, DAZE, & JAMES TOP

Private showing 6-8 pm, invitation only.
Public opening reception 8-10 pm.

info: Marc L.Ent. 212.674.1027/674.4687

*Net profits benefit The Learning Tree

exhibit & information on line at: voiceoftheghetto.com//METALLURGY.htm
>917.721.3131

BUD
DHA
NYC

1999 exhibit of works in spray enamels on metal by New York Subway legends: Kel 1, Stan 153, Part 1, Chain 3, Scotch 79, W est one, Doc TC5, Soe Xmen, Raze & James Top

"You got to get online, you got to get a computer. That's like the easiest step, I think, to getting a lot of information without leaving your house."- Fab 5 Freddy

Supreme, Crash Crew, Push, Fab Five Freddy, Leo, Kev Rockwell at 88HipHop.

DJ Enuff, Push, DJ Mocha Sunflower and King Uprock.

QUEENS, NYC
MAIN SOURCE

THE LARGE PROFESSOR

FRESH! Magazine presents
an evening of

BREAKING, RAPPING & ROCK N' ROLL

THURS. AUGUST 16, 1984

Doors open 9:30 PM

AT THE CAT CLUB 76 E. 13th St.

V.I.P. ADMISSION $8.00 with this invitation

$12.00 at door   o: Ginger Flemming

Performing Live!

THE CAT CLUB FLASHDANCERS
"Beat Street" movie star rocker
ANDY B. BAD
WHBI radio dj/rappers
THE AWESOME TWO
FRESH! GENERATION
Bklyn street dancers
street comedian
ZEROCKS
"Beat Street"
FUNKY FASHIONS
by Charles Erskines
ARTWEAR by Mercurã
THE FUNKATEERS
("Beat Street")
plus rock n' pop singer
SANDY EAGLE
"She's so Different"

Divine of Realism
Master Freestyle Dancer
and Acrobatic

Joseph Johnson
Boogaloo Joe of Realism
(Early eighty's Picture)

Joseph Hamil
Alternative Dancer
of Realism
Specialising in
Acrobotics

BETE
throw up
on the BB

Timothy Norfleet a.k.a. Professor Pop of Realism N.Y.s first organized Lockers, Robot & Electric Boogaloo Dancers/Mimes

Realism 1982

From the Floor Up- The dancers are:Shock-a-Lock (Kevin Porter) Snapshot (Kevin McCrae), Boogaloo Joe (Then Dr.Poppin'Stein)- Joseph Johnson , Professor popp- Timothy Norfleet, Lady Mime- Alicia John

BROOKLYN'S
Fab 5 Freddy

a.k.a.

Freddy B

and

Kid Creole

of the

Furious 5.

Flyer
designed
by
Phase 2

A SURESHOT PARTY PRESENTATION
THURS. JANUARY 21
"AANOTHER DEF BET"
NEGRILL 181
Second   11th & 12th St   Avenue

D.J.
Jazzy Jay
Em Cee
Ikey C

D.J.
AFRIKA
BAMBAATAA
'1 OF THE
ZULU NATION

Guest D.J.s
Whiz Kid
And
Cool Dee

Our Master Of Ceremonies Fab Sive Crews...
Freddy B, roc'shockin' U'all!
•And A Do Or Die Dance Duel•
Rock Steady vs FloorMasters...

DISCO·ROCK·B BEATS & R n B
Mike Loop de loop Holmans
VIDEO SHOW

It
Opens
•11pm
Admissn'
5$

Hey! Make sure we see
your face in this place!
Showtime 12

SURE
SHOT
CREW
$2'

PHASE II

PUSH with New York City's most wanted Graffitti Writters

A United Hip Hop Nation

Talent Show Again Tops in Town!

Seen here in full career of electrifying Robot Dance are members of "Realism" dance trio from Van Dyke Houses. Trio of Kevin Porter, Andre Royall and Shakespeare Newsome took first in 12-17 year category.

The 1981 Trio of Realism

ive at Lincoln Center in New York- Alice Tully Hall
Ir-shock-aLock, Professor Popp, Dr. poppin'Stein

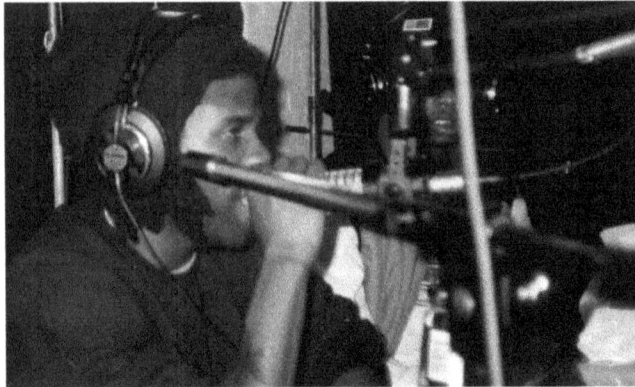
DAS EFX straight from the sewer

DAS EFX

Artist Brett Dizney-Cook sits in front of his piece.

The God Squad (N.O.G.)

IN THE NAME OF
ALLAH

EARLY 1970'S GRAFFITI CREW "THE GOD SQUAD"
CONSISTED OF
MEMBERS OF THE NATION OF GODS AND EARTHS

Super Brooklyn- Cocoa Brovaz

Where BROOKLYN æt?
–B .I.G.

B.I.G..
May 21,1972-March 9,1997

King Uprock, Fast Break and Push

Chic and Push discussing the life and death of BIG

Bronx DJ Grand Wizard at H.O.P. Soul Powers in Brooklyn

Gang Starr from Boston to Brooklyn **R.I.P. Guru**

Fresh Generation Members: Speedy, Frank Swift, Push and Animal

A young Genius-Wu-Tang Clan (Photo: Cold Chillin)

IRON MIKE

BROWNSVILLE

BROOKLYN

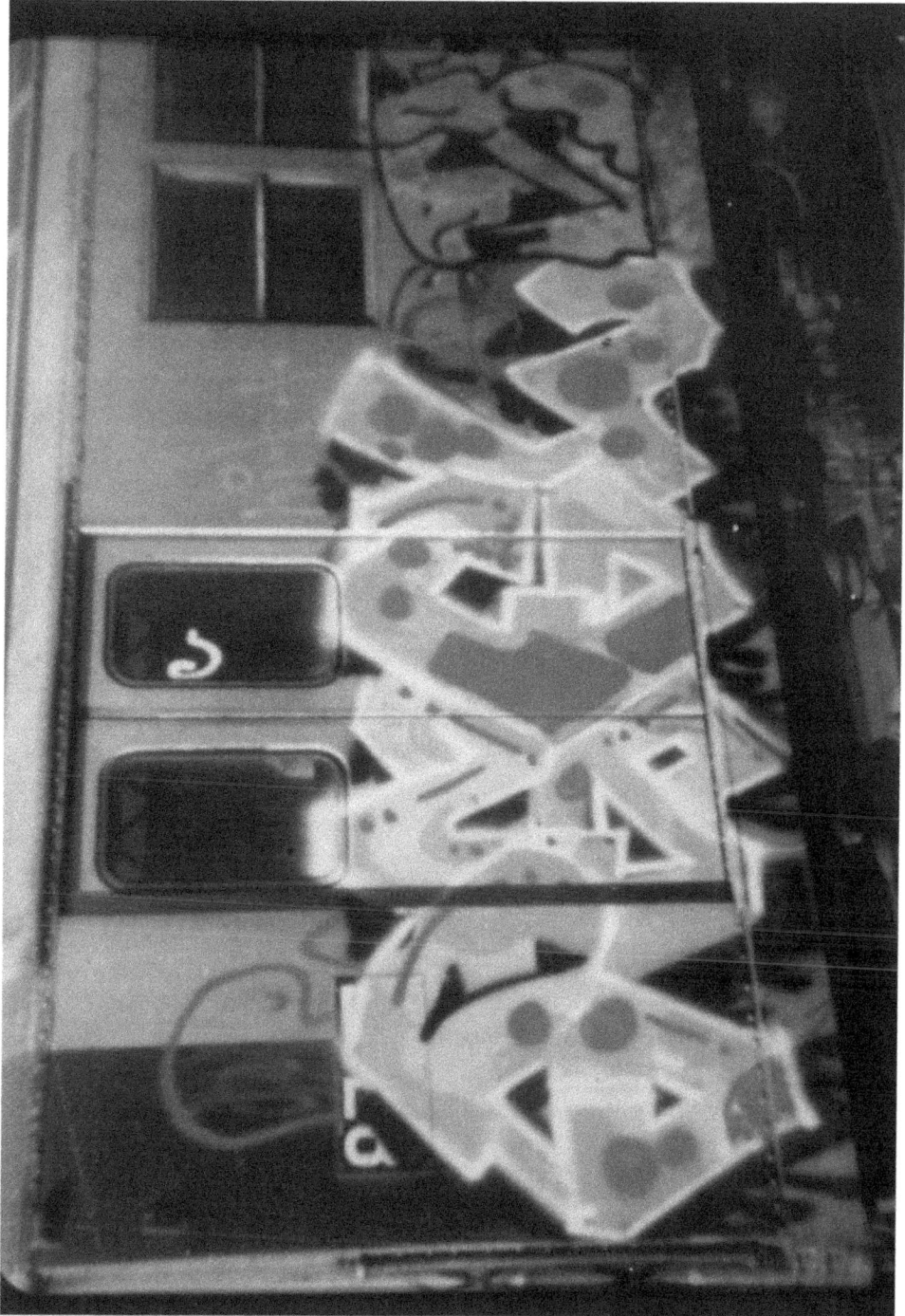

The Chain 3 Collection

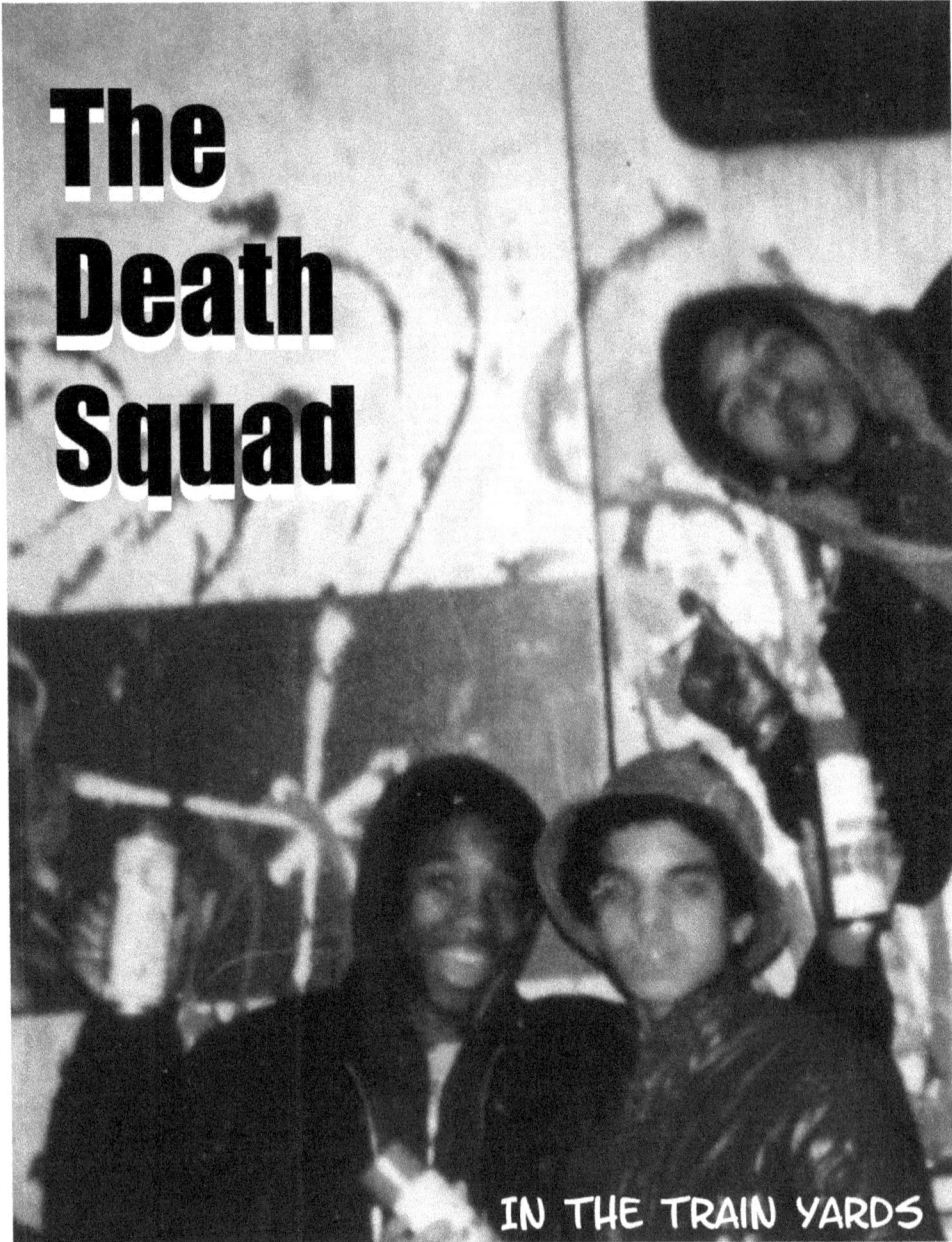

The Death Squad

IN THE TRAIN YARDS

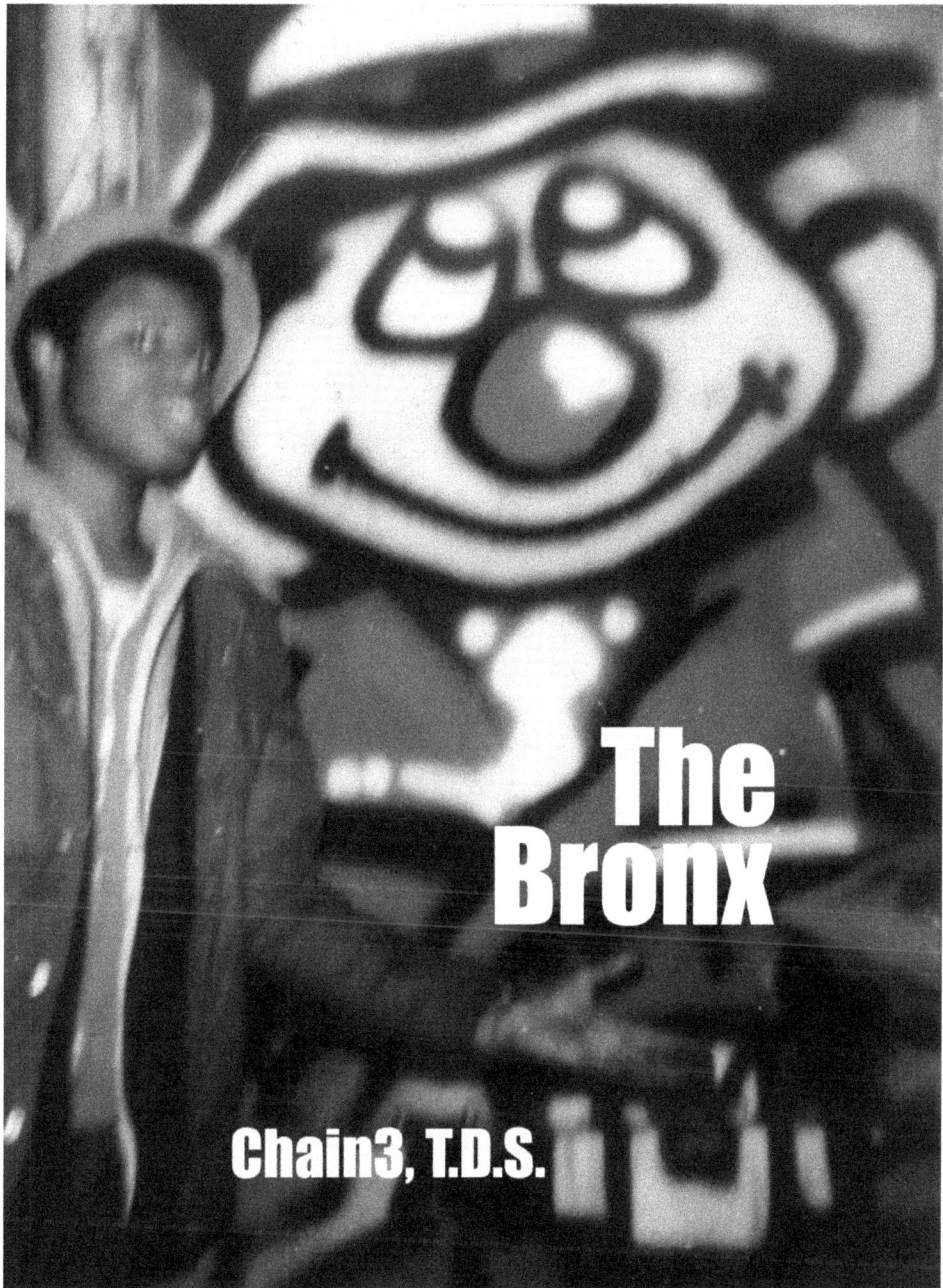

The Bronx

Chain3, T.D.S.

True School

Phase 2, Chain 3 and Bama

Chain 3 in motion

THE BX!

BX ORIGINAL

Chain 3 a Bronx native that hit the subway- 241st Street to Utica

SUPER RHYMES

Celebrates 30
years of Hip Hop

JIMMY SPICER

Winston

PRODUCER SPYDER D ORIGIN: QUEENS

SPARKY-D
Featuring Grand Creator K-WIZ

THE BK BOMBER

MC LYTE

MC SPARKY D
origin: Brooklyn
group: The
Play Girls

MC LYTE
origin: Brooklyn
battle status :
DANGEROUS

THE LATE
GRAND MASTER FLOWERS

Quick Note:
DJ Maboya, Flowers, Pete "DJ" Jones, Undertaker Ash
& Ron Plummers and others are known as New York City
Mobile DJ Foundation.
The Late Grand Master Flowers was from Farragut, Brooklyn.

I'M FROM BROOKLYN

COUNT COOLOUT

Count Coolout recorded
Rhythm Rap Rock on Boss
Records in 1980.

"God Bless Mr. Magic & Frankie"
- Count Coolout

Billy Nichols a musician and producer for the world renown band B.T.(Brooklyn Trucking) Express, produced two of Rap's Greatest story tellers Jimmy Spicer's " The Adventures of Super Rhymes" and James(Count Coolout) Minor "Rhythm Rap Rock". Both men hailing from Brooklyn, NYC, often mistaken for the same person. Minor credits their limited radio air play success to Mr. Magic and the late Frankie Crocker of WBLS "Back then we didn't have music videos, God Bless Mr. Magic & Frankie" said Count Coolout.

MR.MAGIC 1956-2009

BROOKLYN QUEENS

INFINITY & THE PAPER GIRLS

At the age of 13, Infinity known then as Half Note, recorded songs with Big Daddy Kane & was a member of Wu Tang's Proctect Ya Neck family.

T.F.G. ON A BROOKLYN ROOF TOP

Photo Dawoud Bey

Speedy E, Teena, Push, Cris Cross, Frank Swift and Animal

Assemblyman Hakeem Jefferies, Fresh Generation's Teena & Female Graffiti pioneer Cowboy of the EXvandals. at the 2006 Brooklyn Hip Hop History Celebration.

Quick Note:
Newcleus was a 1970's DJ collective known as Jam On Productions. Circuit Breaker's Scott Chester Launched Acid Cigars in 2000.

BROOKLYN ORIGINALS Hip Hop culture

PIONEERS OF THE GAME

Bama, ExVandals co-founder Wicked Gary & Vernon Reid of Living Colour.

East NY, Brooklyn

Fatboys

Aka The Disco 3

Respect to:

DJ UNDERTAKER ASH
RON PLUMMERS
FRANKY D
KC THE PRINCE
OF SOUL
DIVINE SOUNDS
MORTON & BOSSY
NOD SQUAD
THE GOD SQUAD

LOVE FOR THE CULTURE

Radio Air Personality Ken "Spider" Webb

FM RADIO
NEW YORK HIP HOP PIONEERS

1. Mr.Magic
2. Supreme Team
3. DJ Jazzy J
4. DJ Afrika Islam
5. DJ Red Alert
6. Chuck Chillout
7. Hank Love & Dna
8. The Awesome 2

PRE- XCLAN

Professor X & activist Elombe Brathwaite

Recording Artist Super Natural

BIG DADDY KANE

THE 80'S HIP HOP

JAM ON

NEWCLEUS

The Fresh Generation

Mabusha Cooper collection

Speedy E, Teena & Mo of B.S.D.

Brooklyn Street Dancers featured dancers from
every section of Brooklyn. B.S.D. was later renamed
The Fresh Generation, members also included
Poppy Perez, Merissa Gant, Hit Man Slade & Malik Cumbo.

R.I.P.

Cool DJ Law in the Late 1980's
featuring: Jeff Love & Pm Dawn's funky drummer Todd at Soul Powers.

PAULA
PERRY

The Queen of Fort Greene

Paula was an original member
of Masta Ase's The INC.
She also is reported
to have written
Lil Kim first rhymes fo
a Sarah J. High
School play.

FORT GREENE
BROOKLYN

Boro Check: Master Ase was also a Graff writer.

De la Soul 's Plug Tunin was a sample of
Brooklyn's R&B group The *Invitations* "Written on the Wall".

"We live in Brooklyn Baby"
- Roy Ayers

THE INVITATIONS

"Ante up"– Mop

United Brooklyn was a Black & Latino construction coalition spearheaded by the late Sonny Carson.

PUSH SUPER BREAKS

BKLYN Anthems

1) "Sex Machine"- James Brown
2) "Scratchin"- Magic Disco Machine
3) "The Assembly Line"- Commodores
4) "Its Just Begun"- Jimmy Castor
5) "Scorpio"- Dennis Coffey
6) "Rock Steady"- Aretha Franklyn
7) "Do The Funky Chicken"- Rufus Thomas
8) "Super Sperm"- Captain Skky
9) "Good Times"- Chic
10) "Love Is The Message"- MFSB
11) "Shinning Star"- Earth, Wind and Fire
12) "Good Times"- Kool & The Gang
13) "In The Bush"- Musique
14) "Dreaming A Dream"- Crown Heights Affair
15) "Bongo Rock"-The Incredible Bongo Band
16) "Funk To The Folks"- Soul Searchers
17) "Pump It Up"-Trouble Funk
18) "Another One Bites The Dust"- Queen
19) "Catch A Groove"- Juice
20) "Bustin Out"- Rick James

THE MOST WANTED BROOKLYN RECORDS
1) "The Sounds of Brooklyn"- T.S.O.B.
2) "Brooklyn is in the House"- Cut Master DC
3) "Do or Die Bed Stuy"- Divine Sounds
4) "Brooklyn Style"- Choice MCs
5) "Top Billin"- Audio Two
6) "Go Stetsa"- Stetsasonic
7) "No Sleep till Brooklyn"- Beastie Boys
8) "Brooklyn"- MC Lyte
9) "Danger"- Blahzay Blahzay
10) "Brooklyn Takin' Money"- Boostin Kev

1. We Live in Brooklyn Baby – Roy Ayers
2. Bucktown- Smif-n-Wessun
3. Crooklyn- Crooklyn Dodgers
4. The Place Where We Dwell-Gangstarr
5. Brooklyn – Fabulous
6. Brooklyn - Mos Def
7. Brooklyn (go hard) - Jay-z
8. Brooklyn Zoo – ODB
9. Borough Check -Digable Planets
10. Bk Anthem- Foxy Brown
11. Brooklyn - Vybz kartel
12. Lighters Up - Lil' Kim
13. Brooklyn Bullshit- Joell Ortiz
14. 718- Jaz o & Immobilarie
15. What They May Seem -Talib Kweli & Tony Touch

Block Party Anthem
"Love Is The Message"

SOURCES FOR QUOTATIONS

Chain 3, 88HipHop, May 5th, 1999

Chuck D, 88HipHop, June, 1999

Cool DJ Law, 88HipHop, , 1997

Cosmo D, Fast Break, 88HipHop, May 19th, 1999

Flin T.O.P. Push Hip Hop History Video, 1999

Jamil Abdullah Al- Amin (H.Rap Brown) Rally 1968

Marc B, "Steez of Culture" Film, Frontier Production, 1998

Pete DJ Jones, Push Hip Hop History Video, 1999

Popmaster Fable, Black Entertainment Television, original air date
Unknown

Stan153, 88HipHop, May 5th, 1999

Strafe, 88HipHop, May 19th, 1999

Songs

B.I.G. "Where Brooklyn At?

Beastie Boys "No Sleep til Brooklyn"

Blahzay Blahzay "Danger"

Divine Sounds " Do or Die Bed Stuy"

Fat Boys (Disco 3) " Stick em"

Mc Lyte " Brooklyn"

M.O.P. "Ante Up"

Supreme Team "Brownsville/Gods study your lessons"

Thirstin Howl 3rd, "Brooklyn Hardrocks"

Roy Ayers, "We Live In Brooklyn"

PHOTO CREDITS

1. Vanguards (c)1972 Revolutionary
   Woman, Man on the Doorway
   Lolita Standard
2. Dust
   Mabusha Cooper
3. Professor X,
4. Tron
5. Tony Patrick
6. Shock "a" Lock
7. King Uprock (c) 1998
   Rahz Gilmore/ Straw Moore
8. Infinity
   Top of the Line Records
9. Jeff Love
   Jeff Love collection(c)1998
10. Pete DJ Jones and Frosty Freeze
11. Supreme
    Mabusha Cooper (c) 1998
12. Young Push (c) 1972
    Lolita Standard
13. ShaRock, Rodney C,
    Mabusha Collection (c)1998
14. Scotch79, Jamestop, photo by Rahz
15. Young Lil Kim & Mo
    The Barnes Collection (c)1988

16. Brooklyn hard rocks
    Skeeter(c) 1982
17. The Battle
18. Graffiti writers unite
19. Raz1,
20. DJ's unite
21. MC's unite
22. DJ Enuff, Push, DJ Mocha,
    & King Uprock
    Hip Hop History Month 1999 photos
    Rahz Gilmore (c)1999
23. Afrika Bambaataa
    Profile Records (c)1999
24. Bete
    Bete (c)
25. F.A. Posse, Eastern Parkway B-boy
    on the shuttle, David Black (c)1999
26. Realism Photos
    -Shock A Lock-
27. Brett Dizney-Cook Collection
28. Chain 3 Collection
29. Pete DJ Jones Collection

Addition Photos: Wayne Winston. Gary Fritz Collections & Mabusha Cooper Collection
Gary Gant /Lew Kirton Collections

Mabusha "Push" Cooper is best described as a multi -faceted, multi-talented artist whose reach spans across many areas of Hip Hop culture.

He is a former host of 88 Hip Hop, CMGI's least and co-founder of Brooklyn Hip Hop History Celebration (June), Push, Hails from Brooklyn, New York.

A former breakdancer, writer and organizer.

He co-founded Educated Voices of Hip Hop Inc (Educated Voices); ***www.evvh.org*** a community –based coalition which promotes collective building and youth empowerment through Hip Hop culture.

For additional information visit
www.illbrew.com